D0452000

OUTDOOR TALES
——— *of* ———
NORTHEAST OHIO

ANDREW J. PEGMAN

THE
History
PRESS

Published by The History Press
Charleston, SC
www.historypress.com

Copyright © 2021 by Andrew J. Pegman
All rights reserved

Front cover: *Dusk*, by Bob White.
Back cover: Author holding steelhead. *Courtesy of Gareth Thomas.*
Unless otherwise noted, interior images are by the author.

First published 2021

Manufactured in the United States

ISBN 9781467150231

Library of Congress Control Number: 2021945862

Notice: The information in this book is true and complete to the best of our knowledge. It is offered without guarantee on the part of the author or The History Press. The author and The History Press disclaim all liability in connection with the use of this book.

All rights reserved. No part of this book may be reproduced or transmitted in any form whatsoever without prior written permission from the publisher except in the case of brief quotations embodied in critical articles and reviews.

Praise for Outdoor Tales of Northeast Ohio

Here I had thought that the classical outdoor writing of my youth had long vanished, apparently with my youth, and then suddenly while perusing a manuscript by Andrew Pegman I came across it once again. What a delight! Not only were there the struggles of Pegman to catch a large steelhead trout out of the Chagrin River (yes, there is such a river—I looked it up on a map) there is also a toad hopping across his backyard. He gets a few hundred words out of that toad. This is nature writing of a kind I once devoured in my youth, and it was such a pleasure to come across it again in the writings of Andrew Pegman.

Patrick F. McManus,
Circles in the Snow

The world is filled with anglers and outdoorsy types who aspire to write, but there are few truly great authors who can really relate the raw essence of fishing and the outdoors. Dr. Andy Pegman is a master of the writing craft, for sure, but he's also obviously walked many miles in wet boots. He's my favorite type, because his writing is always interesting, real, honest, and inspiring.

Kirk Deeter,
Editor-in-Chief, Trout Unlimited Media
Editor-at-Large, Field and Stream

DEDICATION

I dedicate this book to my son, Andrew; my wife, Amy; my mother, Cynthia; my father, Edwin; my brother, Mike; my sister, Kristen; my grandfathers, John and Owen; my grandmothers, Stella and Kathleen; my cousins and extended family; my friends and colleagues at Cuyahoga Community College; and author Patrick F. McManus.

Beartown Lakes reflections I.

Contents

Acknowledgements   9
Introduction   11

Part I. Tales of My Chagrin
1. The Journey: What I'm After   14
2. Much to My Chagrin, or My First Steelhead on the Fly   17
3. A Tale of Two Trips   20
4. Fishing from Stone   24
5. Saturday Morning   26
6. One Last Cast   28
7. A Whale of a Fish Tale: Trophy Carp   30
8. I Wanted to Catch a Smallmouth Bass…   32
9. A First Fish   33

Part II. A Tip of the Cap to Patrick F. McManus
10. The McManus Effect—Fact or Fiction?   38
11. Tying My Own, Revisited   40

Part III. Tales of Trees and Wings
12. From Birding to Fishing: An Angler Needs to Be Resourceful
    Above All Else   44
13. Birding with My Boy   46
14. Winter Birding Warms My Heart   48

15. Field Notes: Birding Journal — 51
16. Field Notes II: In Living Color — 53
17. The Joy of Winter Birding — 55
18. Downy Woodpecker Down! — 59

PART IV. CONNECTIONS WITH THE EARTH
19. Black Friday the Natural Way — 62
20. On Silence, Peace and Solitude — 64
21. Starfish in Maine — 67
22. On Gardens and Other Simple Pleasures — 69
23. From Little Plants, Mighty Pumpkins Grow — 71
24. Fishing in Greece — 73
25. The Tale of the Toad — 75

PART V. THE KAYAK FISHING STORIES
26. Blind Angler George Tice Clears Hurdles and Gives Back — 78
27. Ten Easy Steps to Properly Catch-Photo-Release a Fish — 80
28. How Kristine Fischer Became a Full-Time Tournament Pro — 82
29. How Fishing for Salmon Shark Started the Big Game Craze — 84
30. Nine Steps to Get into Adventure Fishing — 86
31. The True Value of Fishing Licenses — 89
32. Kayak Fishing Revolution — 91
33. Summer Kayak Catfishing — 93

PART VI. PRO TIPS ON OUTDOOR SKILLS
34. Catch a Steelhead on the Fly — 96
35. How to Fly-Fish for Walleyes at Night — 98
36. Twelve Hot Patterns for Great Lakes Steelhead — 101
37. How to Icefish for Giant Walleye, Lake Trout and Perch — 109
38. Shotgun Safety: A Perfect Fall Day — 113
39. Take Slab Crappies for a Dip — 116
40. Smallmouth Alley — 119

PART VI. CONCLUSION
41. Walking the Line: Finding Summer during COVID-19 — 124

About the Author — 128

Acknowledgements

I am grateful to the following publications for publishing my stories:

"The Journey: What I'm After" first appeared in *SUN Newspapers*.

"Whale of a Fish Surprises Youthful Angler," "An Angler Needs to be Resourceful Above All Else," "Black Friday the Natural Way," "There's Something to be Said for Winter Fishing," "One Last Cast," "On Silence, Peace and Tranquility," "Shotgun Safety: A Perfect Fall Day" and "Steelhead on The Fly: Liskay Offers Pro Tips" first appeared in *Ohio Outdoor News*.

"Winter Birding Warms my Heart" first appeared in the *Ohio Cardinal* 37, no. 2. "Birding with My Boy" first appeared in the *Ohio Cardinal* 38, no. 4.

"Much to My Chagrin," "Tying My Own, Revisited," and "Smallmouth Alley," first appeared in *American Angler* magazine.

"How to Fly-fish for Walleyes at Night," "Twelve Hot Patterns for Great Lakes Steelhead" and "How to Fish for Giant Walleye, Lake Trout and Perch" first appeared in *Field & Stream*.

"Take Slab Crappies for a Dip" first appeared in *Outdoor Life*.

"Fishing from Stone" first appeared in *The Drake*.

"Blind Angler George Tice Clears Hurdles and Gives Back" (Winter 2018), "Ten Easy Steps to Properly Catch-Photo-Release a Fish" (Summer 2019), "How Kristine Fischer Became a Full-Time Tournament Pro" (Summer 2019), "How Fishing for Salmon Shark Started the Big Game Craze" (Early Summer 2020), "9 Steps to Get into Adventure Fishing" (Early Summer 2020), "The True Value of Fishing Licenses" (Fall 2020) and "Kayak Fishing Revolution" (Fall 2020) first appeared in *Kayak Angler* magazine.

"The McManus Effect: Fact or Fiction" and "Walking the Line: Finding Summer During COVID-19" first appeared in *TROUT* magazine.

"Downy Woodpecker Down" was first published in *The House Wren: Bulletin of the Audubon Society of Greater Cleveland* 33, no. 9 (December 2015).

Introduction

Dear Readers:

Welcome!

This book is a collection of stories of fun and adventure in the great outdoors. Although the stories range in location from Maine to Greece, I spend the vast majority of my time outdoors fishing, hiking and birding in Northeast Ohio.

I want to sincerely thank my family for their support, most of all my son, Andrew. This book is for you; I love you so much.

I also want to thank my colleagues and students at Cuyahoga Community College. I have the best job in the world. Finally, I want to thank all the editors who published my stories and John Rodrigue of The History Press. Thank you all for believing in me.

And thank you for reading!

Sincerely,

Andrew Pegman

Part I

TALES OF MY CHAGRIN

Andrew panfishing.

1

THE JOURNEY

What I'm After

The sun was sinking slowly in a brilliant display of golden light, but the clear, cold river yet again refused to yield a steelhead—or anything else. It was a brisk evening on the Chagrin River in Northeast Ohio, and I had plenty of time to enjoy the scenery, though as much as I enjoy the scenery, catching a fish would have been a pleasant diversion. But fishing the Chagrin isn't simply about catching fish—at least, that's what I've told myself. I've fished the Chagrin many times and used almost every conventional fishing method to pluck an elusive fish from its waters. Despite my best efforts, I've had little luck; however, it has become a necessary part of my existence to fish that river—fish or no fish.

Despite its name, the Chagrin River is one of the premier steelhead trout rivers in Ohio. Without question, there are many steelhead in this river. They live and swim there; occasionally, they break the surface of the water, perhaps to prove they exist. Sometimes I break the water's surface too, not to prove I exist, but because of the slick rocks along the bottom that are more slippery than a greased sheet of ice. So, for me, the river could not be more aptly named.

Thoreau once said that "many men go fishing their entire lives without knowing it is not fish they are after." My guess is Thoreau probably wouldn't last ten minutes on the Chagrin. Unless, of course, it was not fish he was after. In that case, the Chagrin would suit him very nicely.

Thoreau, or other such philosophical anglers, may argue that being out in nature is its own reward. Indeed, standing along a pristine river with the

Flyfishing the Chagrin.

water softly gurgling and the air light with fragrant blossoms may rival a religious experience. But I don't fish a pristine river—I fish the Chagrin.

When I fish the Chagrin for steelhead, I do it when the weather is cold and the ground is muddy. I remember one such occasion specifically. The river was clipping along at a terrific pace, and the wind was piercing. It was late November, and it was so cold that the guides on my rod were freezing solid after every cast. When I tried to chip the ice off my rod, my hands were so numb I couldn't make use of my fingers. This is what I am after; this is fishing at its purest.

Yes, it is the pursuit of fish that brings me back to the river. However, the fish that swim in my dreams fight harder than any I have ever hooked. When I stand along the bank of the river, I feel a reawakening of my spirit. It is the spirit of life and living and fishing a river named the Chagrin while fully understanding the irony of that name and the futility of my pursuit. It is the bitterness of the battle that is the true reward.

So, perhaps Thoreau was right, but I will continue to stand along that river until it is only fish that I am after.

2

MUCH TO MY CHAGRIN, OR MY
FIRST STEELHEAD ON THE FLY

It was late November in Northeast Ohio. On a cold and dark morning, a glimmer of sunlight pierced the gray clouds. It was a perfect day to go steelhead fishing. I can explain everything.

I was to meet a group of novice fly-fishing enthusiasts and expert guides to learn how to enhance my steelhead casting, presentation techniques and, hopefully, land a few feisty chromers from a nearby river. I had been fly-fishing for steelhead on my own a few times over the years—OK, a few hundred times—but never with much luck. In fact, my lack of success caused me considerable chagrin, which coincidentally was the name of the river we planned to fish.

I remember years ago looking up *chagrin* in an old encyclopedia, my preferred, and only, search engine at the time. The definition was some combination of distress, failure and humiliation. Although it was unlikely the scholars who penned the definition had fished the Chagrin, their description captured the spirit of most of my outings on the river rather well. Other steelhead anglers seemed to do just fine on the Chagrin, but its fish always seemed to elude me.

Preparation for the trip began weeks in advance. I bought nice, new, insulated chest waders to replace my not-so-nice, leaky, old chest waders. Unfortunately, I didn't try on the new waders before the trip. (FYI, planning has never been my strong suit.) When the morning of the outing arrived, I was dismayed to learn they were a tad large. In fact, they were enormous.

Nevertheless, I put them on in desperation, cramming the additional material into my new wading boots. But the boots were far too small to accommodate the many folds of neoprene designed for a much larger man. Frustrated, I left the new waders in a crumpled heap in the corner of my basement, where they would likely sit until I bought a new house.

With a sigh, I searched out my old waders. There they were, in a heap in an opposite corner of the basement, right where I had left them. I pulled them on, hoping that, over time, their leaks had miraculously improved. But that is not the nature of leaks. As I was running late, I would have to make the best of it, so I threw them in the trunk with my gear.

When I arrived at the river, the other anglers were dressed and outfitted as though prepared for an Arctic expedition. I was wearing a thermal shirt and ball cap. We met in a group and listened as the guides shared years of secret tips and tricks of the sport of fly-fishing. Unfortunately, I had to divide my attention between listening to their instruction and warming my increasingly numb hands. It was quite a bit colder than I expected. (Did I mention planning has never been my strong suit?) This trip was going to be rough.

When the huddle broke and others began to tie on their flies and tinker with their expensive fly rods, I had a singular focus. I quietly retreated to my car to find anything to take the edge off the bitter cold. I rooted through my backseat and came up with an old sport coat, which I found wadded in a heap, a pair of old leather gloves and a threadbare winter hat. I couldn't believe my good fortune, and I happily rejoined the group. Although I did receive a few amused glances at my strange ensemble, I was much warmer.

But I now had a new problem—after all the trouble of finding a warmer wardrobe, I had snapped off the tip of my fly rod closing my car door. One of the more seasoned guides noticed my plight and offered me the use of a gleaming rod and reel. At that exact moment, the sun peeked from above the tree line. I took it as a good omen, accepted the guide's generous offer and felt my spirits brighten. Perhaps this was the day the Chagrin would deliver me the bounty to which I had long aspired.

We trudged single file to the river through a muddy open field after receiving final instructions. We hit the water and spaced out to work different stretches of a nice, deep run. Despite being the least prepared, I was handy with a rod and reel. My casts hit their mark accurately as the other anglers struggled with their presentations. The conversation was good-natured and upbeat, but I was more determined than ever to catch my first steelhead. Our guide, an experienced and excellent fly angler himself, was pleased with my efforts and turned his attention to the other two members of our steelheading trio.

We alternated positions for the first thirty minutes or so, working our way up and down the river, but nobody got a strike. I worked my way back upstream to the top position and felt the increasingly steady flow of ice-cold river water seep through my waders and soak my socks and legs. My level of discomfort shifted from mildly annoying to increasingly painful, and I knew I wouldn't be able to stand in the river too much longer.

Nevertheless, I kept casting. Suddenly, I felt a slight tug and tried to set the hook. Missed.

"I think I had a bite," I called downstream to my partners.

They looked up briefly from their casts and then returned to fishing.

A few casts later, it happened. I had a strike. I set the hook. I saw a flash of silvery chrome swirl beneath the water. The rod doubled over.

"I've got one!" I called. At long last, I thought to myself.

"Let him run," yelled the guide.

Although my heart was pounding, I played the fish skillfully and calmly as it acrobatically broke the water and swam furiously up and downstream. For some reason, I knew I wasn't going to lose the fish. The guide now stood at my side.

"It's a nice one, too," he said.

I worked my way to the bank as the guide got the fish in the net. It was a beauty. It was long, lean and colorful—a nice buck. The fish—and the moment I had been patiently awaiting for almost two decades—had finally come to fruition. It took all my self-control to keep from jumping for joy, but I played it cool. "That's a nice one, huh?" I said.

"It's a beauty," the guide replied.

We took some quick photographs and returned the fish to the water. My fishing partners congratulated me and continued to fish. I made a few more casts, but the cold was getting to me, and in the interest of saving all of my toes, I decided it was time to roll. I returned the rod and reel to the guide with a hug and my sincere gratitude. One of the anglers called out to me, "Oh sure, catch a fish and then bail."

At that moment, a majestic bald eagle soared above the river. The moment could not have been more perfect, and I said a silent prayer of thanks, not just for the fish, but for the experience and for the Chagrin.

"Good luck, fellas," I said, as I made my way back to the field and my car.

I couldn't wait to get those leaky waders off and warm my feet before I succumbed to frostbite. I considered throwing the waders away, but instead, I left them in the trunk. Never know when I might need them again. I then took one last look back at the river and turned the heater on high. I was finally at peace with my Chagrin.

3

A TALE OF TWO TRIPS

I'm staring, transfixed, through the dusty mini blinds of my bedroom window into a bright blue endless sky. The sweet notes of songbirds drift in along with the warm breeze. The fresh air beckons me outdoors. It's time to fish. The river waits.

I hear a faint ringing off in the distance, but the noise gradually fades into the sound of a car engine roaring to life. My tie and briefcase are sitting shotgun as I glance in the rear-view mirror and smile at the sight of my fly rod and new waders. The anticipation of something wonderful can be better than the thing itself. In this case, it's the dream of the perfect fly-fishing trip. It is the dream that keeps me returning to the water time and time again.

The river lies at the north end of an emerald-green field flanked by bluebird boxes at each corner. The bluebirds flit from branch to branch in the large pine trees, welcoming me to the outdoors. The sun is just peeking over the trees, and its light glistens on the dewy grass and wildflowers.

The red-winged blackbirds announce my arrival to the river. I'm mesmerized by the sparkling water—all its intricacies and wrinkles.

My textbook casts are crisp and precise. I drop a perfect cast upstream, and the tiny fly silently lands and glides over deep water above a gentle, rippling current. It's an amazing feeling. Each cast is more effortless than the previous—almost too easy.

I take a moment to read the water and elect to change spots. Gliding through the water with the grace and elegance of a sleek and stealthy trout,

I wade to the edge of a deep pool. Within moments, a fish is on my line, and each fish that follows is larger than the last. I catch and release dozens of healthy and colorful rainbow trout.

Satiated, I briefly pause from my angling pursuits, locate a large flat rock on which to sit and pull a charcoal pencil and sketchpad from my fly vest to make rough drawings of the local flora and fauna for later research. Soaring high above me is a mature bald eagle. Farther downstream, and partially hidden by a fallen tree, a great blue heron stealthily scouts for easy meals along the bank. It pauses to watch me. Suddenly, a swift accipiter pierces through the air and disappears in a flash around a river bend. I can't recall the species in any of my field guides, so I promise to paint a watercolor of it from memory when I return home.

The bright sun continues its ascent into a cloudless blue sky. I tip my cap to the river and decide to return home. It's been a perfect morning. It's one more trek I'll add to the nostalgic recollections of the times I walked through other fields like this one. I am grateful for the warm air, open fields and all the great years of fishing ahead of me. I hop into my car, turn the key and feel the engine roar to life. Time to head home.

Somewhere in the distance, I hear a faint ringing. It's increasing in volume. I reach out and turn the radio volume dial down, but the noise grows louder.

It takes a moment to focus my vision and arrange my bearings. An annoying noise—the same noise I've heard for countless mornings—clangs relentlessly in the darkness. I silence it with a slap, yawn and embrace the silence.

"It was only a dream," I thought.

I stand and stretch my sore back. It's still dark outside. Coffee—I need coffee, but it's not to be. My metal scoop clangs on the bottom of a can of grounds and returns empty, so I'll forsake my ritual today.

I planned to arrive on the water before sunrise, but it's closer to noon when I finally reach the river. Crow calls fill the gray, overcast sky, and the flies are swarming around me. Will the fish be just as eager to bite?

I don an old brown pair of chest waders that aren't branded with any discernable logo. It may be the first time I've worn them. Or, perhaps, at some point, I made a conscious choice never to wear them again. It's difficult to recall.

Deep footprints mark a path across the wet, muddy field. There are no eagles, bluebirds, deep riverside springs or big rock candy mountains here. Riverside, after a careful assessment of all possible options, I reluctantly access the water via a slick, muddy hill. I didn't have much say in that decision—I slip down the steep grade and announce my arrival with a tremendous splash that likely scares any nearby fish far downstream. I regroup enough to assemble my fly rod, attach a fly and gnaw off the knot tag while simultaneously swatting a tap-dancing deerfly on the back of my neck.

The river is running high, and the water is deep—it's so deep I don't see the hole in my path that plunges water halfway up my chest. Water threatens to overrun the top of my waders, but once I gather my footing and take a deep breath, I continue the trek downstream.

I'm not off to a great start, but I see a nice, deep pool that offers hope. I turn the line over a few times to gauge the distance, which I greatly misjudge, and send the offering directly into an overhanging tree twenty feet above the water. The fly returns after a hard yank, along with most of the tree. I free it from its impediments and cast it again.

At long last, my imitation lands on the water, but nothing seems to be hungry, aside from the deerflies and horseflies. No matter—there's a cool, damp sensation around my right knee that now has my attention. The waders are leaking. I'm uncomfortable but ironically pleased I could put the matter of why I hadn't worn the waders for so long to rest.

Overhead, it's hard not to notice the darkening sky, and a slight drizzle turns into a steady downpour. With a thunderous crash, the clouds unleash a torrential fury on the river and my head.

I am soaked, and although I am not prepared for the rain, there's no point going home. There is also no point in running for cover. I can't get any wetter than I already am, and I've long held the notion that fishing is better in the rain.

Across the river, a shaggy great blue heron sits atop a jagged, half-blackened stump and watches me. The wind whips ferociously through the leafless branches, and I'm beyond cold. My fingers, red and numb from the gusts, are difficult to move, but I still manage to quickly gather in my line, check my fly and cast again.

I start to retrieve my fly when there's a hard strike on the end of my line. I set the hook and feel the agitated fury of a mighty trout. I shoot a quick glance at the heron, but it hasn't moved and seems to be enjoying the show from its perch.

As I slowly turn the reel and hold the rod tip high, the wind drives the rain across the river into my face and eyes. I have to squint against the icy spray while the fish leaps and dives for its freedom. Thunder rolls with a rollicking crescendo across the sky. I shut my eyes to keep water out. The darkness is now complete. I can't see anything, but I feel the fish.

The trout jumps as a bolt of lightning rips through the sky, igniting the fish's chrome flanks like a camera strobe. I hold steady. Lightning again splinters the sky and strikes a tree one thousand feet away with a deafening display of sound and sparks. The heron spreads its wings and takes flight, and my line goes slack. The fish is gone.

If there ever was a sign it's time to leave, surely, that was it. I shake my head in disappointment but still can't help but grin. I lost the fish, but that doesn't bother me much. I already imagine my next trip, which will also almost certainly be shuttered by reality. That's all right; storms don't last forever, but dreams never end.

4

FISHING FROM STONE

I'm standing on the breakwall in Cleveland, Ohio. Lake Erie waves are gently lapping against the rocks, and anglers are perched on overturned five-gallon buckets dotting the long structure.

It is here, where stone converges with water, where the weathered rock cuts through the waves to provide lake-fishing access to anglers of all ages. Young and old alike are casting for perch, smallmouth or the occasional steelhead or walleye against the backdrop of the Cleveland skyline. Gulls glide through the air around us, searching for fish. We all converge at this spot, searching for fish.

Fishing from a breakwall is a social act. People are friendly, sharing bait and advice. Most are casting Nightcrawlers or Emerald shiner minnows floating below bobbers or bouncing behind sinkers on the lake floor.

I've been the guy on the bucket many times, fishing with my dad, or my brother or a buddy. Listening to the ballgame on a battery-powered radio and pulling in heavy sheepshead on fat crawlers or catching double-headers of yellow perch on a spreader dangling shiner minnows.

Today, I am the guy with the fly rod, the only guy with a fly rod, casting a hand-tied gizzard shad imitation into the open water, sending my line into the mild chop to find a new way to hook a walleye or a perch, not that I've come close to exhausting the old ways.

So, I am carrying a split bamboo 6wt that may snap if I hook a steelhead or a walleye, but I am not too concerned about that. I tie on a mayfly imitation and send it out as far as I can. A boy stands nearby, watching me retrieve my line. He's holding a weathered Zebco with a large red and white bobber attached to it. I want to say, "I have that rod, too."

I make a few more casts, and then I work my way down to the end of the breakwall. The action is slow, but I get a few smiles and nods. I probably look like I know what I am doing, but I am just casting out into the lake to see what happens, like everyone else. I'm here to enjoy the experience and the brief window of pleasant weather we are afforded in our part of the country before the lake and air turn too cold and fishing the breakwall becomes a distant memory.

Why chase a Lake Erie walleye or perch with a fly rod when other methods may work better? For many, it's the spirit and the challenge of the pursuit. It's also an opportunity to catch different species than Ohio anglers may typically chase with an artificial. For others who don't have boat access or prefer fishing from shore, it's an opportunity to fish a legendary fishery without leaving dry land.

I decide to make one more cast, as every fishing trip ends with one last cast. It would be a great way to end the story with a walleye hammering the fly or a hungry perch lying exhausted at my feet. However, the fly returns untouched, as flies often do.

I'll be out there again. Maybe the next time I'll be on a bucket with a Zebco, watching the guy at the end of the breakwall casting his fly into the lake and landing a trophy walleye. I may stroll down to see what he was using and learn a few things, too.

But I will continue my quest to land a trophy walleye or a fat jumbo perch on the fly. Sometimes it's about the journey, not the destination, so I'll be out there again, sharing the breakwall and hoping for the best.

5

Saturday Morning

The beautiful Saturday mornings in July were passing by too quickly one summer, and I felt anxious that I had not yet seized one yet and made it my own. So, one morning, I threw my fishing rod in the trunk of my car and sped down to the river. I wanted to arrive before the sun did.

I parked in a small gravel lot alongside a large field of tall grasses and wildflowers. Indeed, the morning sun was just peeking over the pines, and the breeze carried the songs of happy birds and buzzing bees.

Sunlight and shadows.

As I made my way down to the river, the blue jays took positions above me to announce my presence. The sun shone brilliantly on the river and illuminated it. I took a tenuous position along the slippery riverbank; I began to cast upstream and let the bait gently glide into the deeper water.

I wasn't having much luck, so I began hiking upstream until I came to the place where I usually catch fish. This morning, the fishing was good. I caught and released six feisty smallmouth bass. They were all on the small side, but they were fun to catch and release.

I saw some interesting wildlife, too. I spotted a many songbirds, dragonflies and damselflies, frogs and turtles and a sleek accipiter flying downstream along the river. Despite my best efforts, I couldn't definitively identify it in any of my field guides. It will likely remain as one of the mysterious outdoor encounters that leave me wondering.

Overall, it had been a splendid summer morning. As I walked back to my car, I felt the heat of the sun on my shoulders and the cool, damp grass on my feet. It was a morning I would not forget.

6

ONE LAST CAST

About a decade ago, the fishing season ended for me only when the river had frozen solid. I would bundle up in those days, throw my gear in the back of my old Jeep and head out to try my luck for winter steelhead. This was a period in my life when I went fishing almost every single night. Many evenings on the river passed uneventfully, but one evening was different.

It was a bright and brisk December day, but it was cold. The frigid water of the Chagrin River swirled and churned as I waded toward a small pool and cast my line upstream. There wasn't a soul to be seen; I was out there alone, trying for steelhead again.

I experimented with a variety of baits—none of which worked—but nevertheless, I tried. I was using a minnow pattern on a small hook that hung a few feet below a lighted bobber on this particular evening. The bobber shone red and bright and left a trail of glowing light against the dark current. I made cast after cast without any luck.

After what seemed like a few thousand casts, I was about ready to give up and head home. After all, it was getting pretty dark, and standing in an Ohio river in December is not exactly soothing—even in waders.

So, as always, I decided to make "one last cast" about a dozen or so times when suddenly my line pulled tight. Naturally, I assumed I had snagged my bait along the bottom of the river. I gave a tug, and it held fast. Oddly enough, it seemed to tug back. An ember of hope began to glow in my mind and light up my eyes. Was this the actual last cast that would finally produce a fish?

I held fast, tugged a bit and again felt some pull in return. Part of me felt like I had a fish on the end of the line, but the other, more rational part

Big moon.

of me knew that I did not. It is not at all uncommon to snag a hook in the Chagrin, so I tried to play the snag to pop it loose.

It didn't pop loose, though; in fact, it seemed to pull harder. My rod tip bent, but there was no left-to-right motion. In other words, if I was hooked up, the fish wasn't budging. This struggle had gone on for twenty minutes or so, and I began to grow impatient and increasingly convinced that there wasn't anything on the end of my line except perhaps a submerged tree branch or an old boot.

Still, I could not bear to potentially lose a fish of this size. If there was a fish on the line, it was a monster. It was starting to get late and bitter cold. Darkness settled in around me. The sun was gone, but I was willing to stay all night.

Finally, just as my thoughts turned to leaving, a huge splash emerged from the very spot where my bobber lit the current. A massive steelhead trout broke the surface of the water, and the tight pressure I had felt in my rod went slack. It was a moment that I can see today, something that I can replay in slow motion in my mind, but in reality, it happened in an instant. There was a fish on the end of the line—a legendary fish. But it wasn't to be. The line had snapped. The fish was gone.

I swore to find it.

7

A WHALE OF A FISH TALE

Trophy Carp

Not all my fishing tales end in woe. There have been many times when I collided with nature and emerged victorious. This was one such time.

I was around fourteen or fifteen, and I was fishing the Chagrin River for carp of all things. The carp that hung lazily in the pools of the Chagrin were massive and fought hard. The carp gets a bad rap because of its appearance—and it truly is a hideous fish—but in those days, it was less about looks and more about action.

A friend and I walked several miles down to a stretch of river that always produced carp. First, of course, we stopped at the grocery store to pick up a few cans of sweet corn. It was the perfect bait—meaning it was cheap and there was plenty of it. The trick was to thread the corn along the hook and line, and then the slovenly carp would suck the kernels up from the bottom of the river. If that doesn't sound that appealing, I guess that's why the term *bottom feeder* is not exactly considered a compliment. We did not discriminate, though—any fish was a good fish.

I had a nifty little ultralight spinning combo that I used to catch everything from bluegill to bass in those days. I fished with it for many years before it finally broke and was retired to the corner of the garage, worn but not forgotten.

So, we sat along the bank, which consisted primarily of dirt and a little mud, and fished away the lazy afternoon in the hot July sun. Looking back, those long summer days were beautiful and endless. Days seemed so long, hours like days, and an eternity to fill before school began again in the fall.

We fished well. Each of us caught a few nice-sized carp and released them. I had just taken a bite of a bologna sandwich that I'd packed for lunch when my rod nearly jerked into the river. I threw down my sandwich and snatched up the rod; I felt a massive fish on the other end of the line. The carp fought hard, but this was no ordinary carp. This fish was a whale.

Time stood still as I wrestled the brute on the end of the line. Unbelievably, my rod and reel held up quite well. It bent but did not break. The fish fought violently, shaking its head to dislodge the hook. It went upstream, downstream. It thrashed about the surface and sank to the bottom like a stone. It didn't matter; I thwarted every move. Steadily, I cranked the reel and gained more ground. This fish was coming ashore.

The entire fight lasted close to thirty minutes. Finally, I maneuvered the great fish to the edge of the bank. It was so big that I had to jump in the water, scoop it up into both of my arms and heave it onto the shore. It was an unbelievably colossal fish.

My friend and I stood admiring the grandeur of this water beast, and after a few minutes, I decided that this was a keeper. It was exhausted and spent and would not have survived even had I released it. Yes, this carp was coming home with me.

So, we began walking home along a busy stretch of road. Cars honked, and men hollered incomprehensibly out of their windows as we walked like storybook characters from a Twain novel, carrying this massive carp.

My mom soon came to pick me up and was undoubtedly thrilled to haul both the fish and me back home, but there was no discussion. I think we all understood the importance of this moment.

8

I Wanted to Catch a Smallmouth Bass...

One morning, on a whim, I packed my rod and reel and took a quick jaunt out to try my hand at some smallmouth fishing. The sun was shining brightly, and as I made my way along the dirt path lining the bank, I saw a beautiful bald eagle flying just above the river. I took that as a good omen.

I found a decent spot and began fishing. As usual, I wasn't having much luck, so I decided to walk upstream. I took note of a few black dragonflies and some pretty songbirds along the pathway. The part of the Chagrin where I fish is absolutely covered in poison ivy this time of year, and I am an annual sufferer of this malady. I get a terrible case of it every year. It's a price I'm willing to pay—even though I hate it.

I was wearing polarized glasses, but it was easy to see how low and clear the river was even without them. I finally found a deep pool and worked my way over to the bank.

I was standing about fifteen feet above the river and having a terrible time trying to cast into the pool. Tree branches seemingly kept reaching out to snag my line. While I was untangling my line from some overhanging leafy branches, I saw a couple of big fish swimming nearby. I was pretty sure they were smallmouth bass.

I cast forty or fifty times, and finally, one of them hit the bait. I set the hook, and it was on. It thrashed and cleared the water several times before it began to tire and give way. The fish fought hard, but I fought harder. I kept my rod tip high and landed it. It was a very nice smallmouth bass.

The fish measured just shy of a Fish Ohio award. Nevertheless, it's one of the best fish I've pulled out of the Chagrin in a long time. Sometimes impulsive, unplanned trips make for the best days on the river.

9

A First Fish

The slow crunch of gravel beneath our tires in the empty parking area signals our arrival at Cuyahoga Valley National Park in Ohio. The sound of one car door closing is followed by another as I emerge with my four-year-old son on a mission to get him his first fish. The sun shone brightly in the clear blue sky.

We are going for a long hike this time, the longest we've ever taken together. I packed our lunch and water in a backpack. I held two fishing rods in one hand and my son's hand in the other. We embark on the trail, a father and son holding hands, walking together. Around us were two magnificent tree swallows, iridescent in the sun, soaring and diving.

The raucous chorus of toads from the vernal pools mixes with the trill of the red-winged blackbirds providing plenty of background music as we make our way along the trail. My son, Andrew, excitedly chatters about catching his first fish.

We step out into the saturated grassland, and my booted feet sink deeply into the mud, emerging with a satisfying squish. Soft feathers from a mourning dove lie scattered at the edge of a pine stand. I hear my son's voice asking:

"Is that bird OK?"

"I think so, son."

The sun grows brighter and warmer, and the songs of nature become louder. A concerned mother robin tracks us nearby.

As we turn around the bend, we see flashes of color: a cardinal, a blue jay and a goldfinch. A red-tailed hawk perches on a bare limb surveying the small lake from the other side of the trees.

A small downy woodpecker plays percussion on a dead stump.

Andrew with a largemouth bass.

"What's that red bird on that bush?"

"That's a cardinal," I say, not really looking.

But it's not a cardinal. I look again. With binoculars this time.

It's brilliant. "It's a scarlet tanager!" It is deep red and flies off like an ember escaping from the fire we built the night before.

A great find. High five!

Our socks are soaked. Not just wet—soaked. We keep going.

We reach the edge of the lake, and I start to rig up the rods. I hand my son my trusty old Zebco, and after a few tries, he casts his nightcrawler out a few feet. It lands with a satisfying plop in the water.

It doesn't take long before his red-and-white bobber starts to dance on the surface of the water.

"You're on!" I say.

"I'm on!" he yells. He laughs as he fights the beast to the shoreline.

"You got a largemouth bass!"

He grins with pure joy as we unhook and gently release the small bass. "Smile!"

It was perfect. Another high five and the moment became a memory that will last a lifetime.

Andrew looks at me and says, "Let's catch another one."

I smile and put on another crawler. Out it whizzes, landing with a big plop. The bobber starts to dance on the surface.

Part II

A Tip of the Cap to Patrick F. McManus

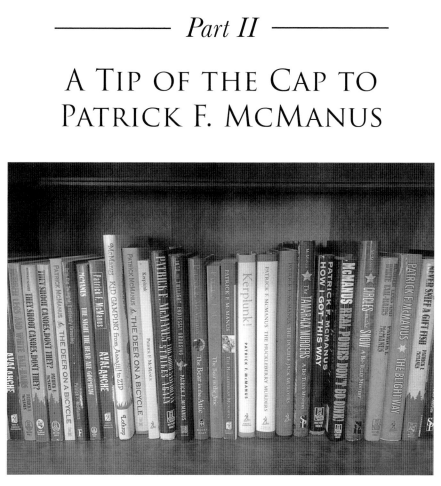

Patrick F. McManus books.

THE MCMANUS EFFECT

Fact or Fiction?

I am standing on the muddy banks of the Chagrin River. The Chagrin is an aptly named river that could have run through fictitious Blight, Idaho, but instead is in real-life Northeast Ohio. In my right hand, I am holding an old split bamboo fly rod. In my left, I am placing a copy of *A Fine and Pleasant Misery* into my fishing bag. I am here today to experiment and do some field research. The title of my study is "The McManus Effect: Fact or Fiction?" The methodology is questionable. The background of the study and the results follow.

My faithful research assistant is my son, Andrew. He is four years old and encouraging me to catch an octopus. Although I explained that the octopuses do not run until fall in Ohio, he is already off chasing a dragonfly that landed on a nearby stone.

Patrick F. McManus was a hero to me and many others who share a love of laughter and a love of the outdoors. Pat's stories had such a significant influence on me that I wrote my master's thesis in English on his works when I finished grad school. The topic was a comparative analysis titled "Man vs. Nature: Tragic vs. Humorous Approach." I compared Hemingway and Faulkner's hunting and fishing stories to McManus's. It was an excellent thesis; I know this because, after he read it, Pat wrote me a letter and told me so himself.

After Pat passed away in April 2018, the entire outdoors world suffered a profound loss. I wanted to write a tribute to him in some way. His stories intertwined with so much of the journey of my own life.

Then I had another idea. I decided to test the McManus Effect. Through his self-deprecating style of humor, Pat always made it seem that he wasn't much of an angler. Many of his stories focused on his uncanny ability to slow down even the best fishing when he hit the water.

So, I tied on a fly that once belonged to Pat McManus, given to me by Pat himself. I knew I was taking a considerable risk, as that fly was one of my prized possessions. To lose it on a snag would be devastating. To lose it on a fish would be slightly more palatable yet far less likely.

Nevertheless, I had to test the theory.

With my son by my side, I sent the McManus fly into the center of the river. It was a decent cast. Then in a flash, it happened! I realized I wasn't going to catch a fish on this fly. (I borrowed that line from Pat. Please consider that admission my citation.) I made a few more attempts, but it was not to be. It seemed the McManus Effect was true after all, but I was too afraid of losing the fly to keep trying.

I looked down and smiled at my son as he worked feverishly pulling each item from my fishing bag and tossing them around the bank. Just as I was marveling at the speed at which he was able to create an incredible mess, he pulled a book from my fishing bag and looked at it.

"Dad," he said, "What's the name of this book?"

"It's called *A Fine and Pleasant Misery*," I replied.

"Oh. Can you read it to me?"

"I would love to."

We gathered up our gear, and I tucked the McManus fly into my shirt pocket. It didn't get me a fish, but the McManus Effect was true. In fact, it gave me something far more significant than I can ever fully articulate.

I held my son's small hand, and we walked into the twilight toward the car together, dreaming of a record octopus run that fall.

11

TYING MY OWN, REVISITED

For my birthday last year, my brother, Mike, gave me a variety of fly-tying materials. The wrapping paper depicted an angler hooked up with a large trout; I tore the paper open, and a package of black bear hair, a peacock feather and other assorted fly-tying items fell onto my lap.

"It's time you started tying your own," he said.

I looked wistfully at the package of black bear hair in my hand. "Yeah…"

Immediately, I was reminded of the legendary writer Pat McManus's story "Tying My Own," a humorous look at the art and challenges of fly tying as only McManus can do it.

I developed a friendship and correspondence with Pat and his family over the years. To the sadness of his many fans and admirers, Pat passed away in April 2018. However, his family shared with me that Pat tried to tie his own flies with little success. In a great story about art imitating life, Pat's daughter Peggy told me that Pat had some experience tying flies.

According to Peggy, and confirmed by Bun (Pat's wife), "I don't recall that he had much skill at tying flies or did it for very long. He bought all the stuff to do it, made a handful of ugly flies that scared all the fish away, and then gave all the supplies to my sister. She started tying flies to make earrings, which she tried to sell through a small business called 'Allurings.' Needless to say, that idea didn't fly either."

I thought back to my own experience tying flies. Now fully reveling in nostalgia, I recalled the time, the only time, I had tied and fished my own fly many years ago. I was around fourteen or fifteen years old, and I had just received my first fly rod and reel. It was a nifty lightweight beginner combo and came with a small, compartmentalized plastic box featuring six different flies.

I fished it every chance I got and wore the bluegill out on my grandma's farm pond dropping Black Gnats on the placid surface of the water. Watching the hungry 'gills gobbling the flies from the surface rather than dunking a red-and-white bobber added a whole new dimension to fishing for me. It was heaven.

Eventually, all six flies were lost, and I needed a fresh supply of artificials, as I was going to the river to fly-fish for smallmouth. So I did what every fly angler does at some point: I decided to tie my own.

At that time, my fly-tying materials were whatever I could find in my house. I started with a small hook, different colored spools of thread from my mother's sewing basket and parts that I removed from old, unused lures in my tackle box.

I decided to make a bee pattern; I do not recall why. I deftly wove black and gold thread around the hook. Around and around. And then around again. I removed two wings and four tiny rubber legs from a few poppers, and voila! I had a truly hideous fly. But would it fish? Unlikely, but I aimed to find out.

The following day, we arrived at the Chagrin, a local aptly named river in Northeast Ohio, and I sent my bee imitation into a deep pool. It sank like a stone.

I understood that this would take a bit more finesse, so I dried it off on my shirt and flipped it out again. I worked it through the water. Bam! It happened. A smallmouth smashed my bee, and I landed it. It was not a football-sized smallie, but it was a pretty fish. I quickly let it go, and it swam away no worse for wear. The fly did not fare as well in battle. All that remained was a loose tangle of soaked thread hanging loosely around a gold hook, but it had done its job.

I took a moment to reflect on the victory of catching a fish on a hand-tied fly. It was unbelievable. My brother was in awe.

"What the hell is that thing on the end of your line?" he asked, looking at the remains of my fly.

"Bee imitation," I said.

He gave me a quizzical look, but moments later, I saw him looking through his fly book for anything resembling a bee.

"I don't have one," he said after a few minutes of fruitless searching.

"That's too bad," I replied. "You should really consider tying your own."

Part III

TALES OF TREES AND WINGS

Magee Marsh boardwalk entrance.

12

FROM BIRDING TO FISHING

An Angler Needs to Be Resourceful Above All Else

Initially, I was going birding, not fishing; however, the small river that ran alongside the woods I was hiking changed my plans. The dense pine forest provided a nice canopy of relief from the hot July sun, and I had already spotted a red-winged blackbird, an eastern bluebird and a Baltimore oriole within the first twenty minutes of my hike.

As I made my way toward the bank of the river to get a closer look at a great blue heron, I noticed a few fish surfacing to take flies. Almost immediately, my desire to fish outweighed my desire to bird, although I hadn't brought any fishing gear. Then it occurred to me that I wanted to try to catch a fish without any of my own gear. Since I already had so many experiences not catching fish when I had brought my own gear, I thought this little experiment would be a refreshing change of pace. So, I made up my mind to fish with whatever I found in the woods and along the river. I put my birding binoculars away and got to work.

Since I had no knife or tools to speak of, I first tried to find a long branch that would make a suitable rod. After ten minutes of hiking around, I spotted a thin, sturdy branch that seemed stout enough to hold a fish. In fact, it proved stout enough to hold a man, but it was also attached to a large tree and, despite my best efforts, had no intention of moving from its fixed position. So, I decided that I better find a fallen branch, and before too long, I did. I pulled the small twigs from the branch and soon had a serviceable twelve-foot pole. Next, I needed some line.

I am aware of various methods of braiding vines or plant fibers to make line. While I appreciate those techniques, I thought it would be easier to use the discarded monofilament that I found sitting in a tangled mess along the shore instead. As I began the tedious ordeal of untangling the line, I had my next stroke of luck—at the end of the line was a small snap swivel attached to a shiny little hook! I thought that I would have had to wade into the river to check submerged logs for snags, but instead, all I had to do was use what another angler discarded. I felt reasonably confident that simply walking along the riverbank for a mile or so in each direction would probably provide me with enough tackle to fish for a week. But I only needed to fish for a day.

I spent the next five minutes or so carving a small notch near the top of my rod with a sharp, jagged stone I found so I could attach and tie the line. What I wound up with was something resembling a crudely made cane fishing pole. In no way could what I made be called a fishing "rod." (Please note the distinction.) I made a few practice casts and didn't have much trouble swinging the hook into the water. The pole was poorly crafted but functional.

Next, I had to find some bait. Any fisherman who has fished as long as I have—and has spent as much time looking for bait as I have—knows where to find worms. I immediately headed to the nearest and largest rocks and logs I could find. After overturning a few, I had a half-dozen red worms. I put them in my shirt pocket and sprinkled a bit of dirt over them, smiling at my resourcefulness.

Now all I had to do was find a suitable little pool to cast my bait. As I clambered through a rather large patch of poison ivy, I found a nice, deep spot to try out my new outfit. I threaded the worm onto the hook and cast it right into the middle of the pool. I kept the rod tip high, making the little worm dance below the surface of the water, and before I knew it, I was snagged. Fortunately, I was able to salvage my hook but lost the worm. I threaded the next one on and tried again

Suddenly, I felt a slight tug. Then another. Then I felt the satisfying pull of a fish. I gently set the hook—I had it. The rod creaked and lightly splintered but stayed intact. Then, like a man operating the arm of a large crane, I maneuvered the fish over to the shore until I could get it into my hand. It was a meaty creek chub but a fish nevertheless. I admired it for a moment and then unhooked it and let it swim free. I accomplished my goal.

On my way back, I propped my homemade rod against a large tree—just in case another birder came along.

13

BIRDING WITH MY BOY

M y son, Andrew, was only two weeks old when he had his first birding experience. On New Year's Day 2015, I poured myself a hot cup of coffee and put my son on my lap as we started our first birding adventure together on that cold Ohio morning.

I pointed out juncos, woodpeckers, cardinals, chickadees, nuthatches and a few other feathered cold-weather companions as he slept quietly in my arms. The hearty little birds were regular winter visitors to our feeders and suet blocks, but we saw them all through the glass of our warm living room.

This past weekend, I had the pleasure of taking my now eight-month-old son to the North Chagrin Reservation for an outdoor birding excursion. As we strolled around Sanctuary Marsh together, we felt the warm early morning August sunshine on our faces as we spotted finches, ducks, herons, swallows, thrushes and geese.

The vibrant and lush sights of nature left my son wide-eyed, seemingly in awe of the intense color and spectacle of the natural world around us. He rode along in his stroller, making soft noises and looking up at the bright sky and across the shimmering water.

I don't know if my son will love nature as much as my wife and I do, but it is important to us that he experiences the world that exists outside of screens, and I don't mean window screens. He and I hiked the same path that I hiked with my father and grandfather. I saw my twelve-year-old self crouched low by the edge of the water, trying to get a better look at a majestic great blue heron.

Andrew looking
for wildlife.

As I walked along with my son, I thought about the mornings that he and I could spend spotting birds and returning home with our socks soaked with morning dew and big smiles on our faces. The best days of my youth and the fondest memories of my childhood all occurred outdoors. It served as the stage for a great many childhood adventures, and although no photographs exist, those days are painted in my memory as idyllically as though they were drawn by Norman Rockwell.

Like most parents, I wonder what the future will hold for my son and the generation of children that grows up with him. I am thankful that I grew up in a time before cellphones and social media stole so much of our precious free time and attention.

After walking a few more laps lost in nostalgia, my mind turned back to what I had been missing. Instinctively, I pulled my smartphone out of my pocket and turned it off. Then I looked up at the blue sky and then down at my son. At that moment, a tiny goldfinch alit right in front of us, its bold, bright plumage striking, and I felt an overwhelming sense of gratitude. I knelt down next to my son and held his small hand so we could look at it together.

14

WINTER BIRDING
WARMS MY HEART

It is late November in Northeast Ohio, and the temperature reflects it. The air is cold, and the wind is whipping the last few leaves off the branches. Fortunately, I am still inside my warm home, but I won't be for long. I reach for my ceramic mug; the coffee is strong and very hot. I take a sip and open the blinds. For a long moment, the wind stops, and there is only stillness, the darkness outside.

Almost magically, a buck materializes from a neighboring woodlot, seemingly from nothingness. It takes a step and then pauses and surveys its surroundings. Then, for reasons known only to it, the massive buck puts its head down and makes a right turn onto my winding suburban street, running as if its very life depends on it. The cold clacking of its hooves beats out a staccato message against the hard pavement, and the sound echoes through the empty air. Moments later, the buck retreats sharply back into the woods. I look up and see a hawk perched on the limb of a massive sugar maple, watching the buck disappear. The noble hawk lets out a piercing cry and takes flight. Nature always speaks if we only listen.

But I did not awaken before the sun on this cold day to gaze reflectively through my kitchen window; I am going winter birding. I set my empty coffee mug down and begin the process of getting ready. First, I climb into my thermal gear. The hardwood floor is cold, but the woods will be much colder. I add a second pair of socks and slide into my lucky fishing sweater. I don't know why it's lucky; I never catch any fish when I wear it. Plus, I'm

Hiking at Swine Creek.

not going fishing. Nevertheless, it's the warmest sweater I own, so it's the right choice.

After gathering enough gear to survive in the wilds for several decades, I am finally ready to depart. As always, I am heading to the deep forest near the Chagrin River. As always, I am departing roughly three hours later than I had initially intended. As always, I will return home half-frozen. Old habits are hard to break.

Winter birding in Ohio is a different kind of birding. It is not for everyone. Some would argue that it is not for anyone, but I disagree. It does require a bit more preparation than the average birding excursion, but with careful planning, that time can be minimized. For example, the process of getting dressed for winter birding, if done correctly, should only take about four times as long as the actual trip. I always try to reach my destination by late morning, say 1:00 or 2:00 p.m. Every birder must stand rigidly by his or her code, especially in adverse conditions.

Because it can get so cold, it can be tough to spend too many hours outdoors during the unforgiving Ohio winters.

But even if the birding time is short, the memories are long. I have seen some remarkable things while winter birding. I have seen golden sunlight gleaming on frozen treetops against a clear blue sky. I have witnessed the

Icy blue lake.

silence of an open forest, and I have seen fellow birders, hearty companions, rubbing their cold hands and warming their hearts by sharing laughs and stories. I've even seen a few birds.

Honestly, winter birding is not for everyone, but there is a great outdoors outside our frozen doors. The winter's cold embrace awaits us.

15

FIELD NOTES

Birding Journal

BOBOLINK | Spotted in a grassy field. Flits from spot to spot. Constant movement.

EASTERN BLUEBIRD | Spotted along the bank of the Chagrin River. Alit on a broken tree branch beside me. Brilliant blue plumage contrasts with white and orange.

BLACK-THROATED BLUE WARBLER | Spotted near a small creek. Beautiful species of warbler. Striking black, white and blue colors. A rare treat.

Black-throated blue warbler.

Mallards taking flight.

MALLARDS | Spotted taking flight on an icy lake. Familiar friends. Often seen in pairs.

RED-TAILED HAWK | Spotted soaring above the Chagrin River. Noted the distinctive tail. Piercing cry.

PILEATED WOODPECKER | Spotted in a patch of pine forest. Hunting for insects. Noise echoes through the woods.

BLACK-CAPPED CHICKADEE | Spotted multiple times in multiple places. Friendly, social birds. On a few hikes, some were just an arm's length away.

BARRED OWL | Hoots heard on a twilight hike, but unseen. Identified the call, which is memorable. Active at night.

16
FIELD NOTES II

In Living Color

When I visit a forest, or a river, or even a field, I engage it with all my senses. Each small component that makes up the whole of nature is equally amazing. My footsteps on a worn path in the woods are as meaningful and revealing to me as the pages of a treasured book.

On a rainy and humid summer night in July, my wife, Amy, and I visited the North Chagrin Metroparks and were treated to multiple interesting bird sightings. For some reason, we were the only two people there, but the summer woodland and wetland creatures were out and about.

PICKEREL FROG | We saw a small pickerel frog sitting on the muddy edge of a puddle that formed along the path. It was, perhaps, five hundred feet away from the river. I bent down to photograph it and was able to hold it in my hand. I set it back down and headed toward the bank of the river, thinking about the creatures that thrive where land and water meet.

GREEN HERON | This was a first sighting for us. Of course, we heard it before we saw it. Its call resembles some manner of war shriek. (Not all birds sing like canaries.) The heron perched down on a wooden fence nearby to scold us, and I was able to get some nice photos and even a short video of the vocal fellow.

GREAT BLUE HERON | I have seen many great blue herons, particularly because I like to fish in rivers. I have written and published both factual and creative stories about them, and they are amazing creatures. On a recent fly-fishing trip, the instructor told us that if you want to fish well, watch the heron and do what he does. Of course, he probably meant with a fishing rod as opposed to a beak, but you get the idea.

American goldfinch | We love finches. They are small, delicate and beautiful. We have a feeder outside our kitchen window and are often treated to the sights of small red house finches and bright yellow goldfinches dropping by for a snack.

Shadowy silhouette of an unknown bird | On the same trip that we saw the green heron, we also saw a bird's silhouette at the top of a tree. I was not able to identify the bird. Part of the fun of birding is discovering the mystery of unknown birds.

17

The Joy of Winter Birding

One December morning a few years ago in Northeast Ohio, my wife, Amy, and I were on a winter hike when we saw our first bald eagle in the wild. The eagle was perched on the bare limb of a massive sycamore tree, surveying a stretch of river. The sleek eagle swooped down to the water, grabbed its prey and took flight against a bright blue December sky. Amy and I looked at each other in amazement. Two things happened that day: we got hooked on winter hiking, and we got hooked on winter birding.

Getting to know and identify the familiar and rare feathered visitors to your area is a rewarding hobby that can bring joy at any age and can even develop into a lifelong obsession. Spending time outdoors to spot and identify birds is an adventure, and winter is the best season to get started. J. Drew Lanham, American author, poet and wildlife biologist, shares some tips for winter birding:

- Winter birds are easier to spot and identify.
- Some familiar birds become more striking in the winter.
- Naming birds is important, but don't worry about that right away.

You can start by hiking your local parks or even strolling around your block. Winter birding is a great opportunity to look more closely at nature while getting the added benefits of fresh air and exercise.

Common redpoll and Lapland longspur.

Once you know and identify the common birds around you, you can begin to have fun seeking rare species and identifying uncommon visitors to your area.

Winter birds can be rare: Winter is a time when rare species come to visit. An urban area, downtown Cleveland has become a landing spot for arctic snowy owls, which hunt the vast expanses of lakefront. My young son and I watched a snowy owl take flight this winter on a bitterly cold afternoon, and it was one of the most memorable moments of my life.

You'll know if you see a snowy owl, but it's OK if you can't name all the birds that you see. I know I can't. Being able to identify birds correctly is important, but don't worry about that right away. Field guides, birding groups and apps can help with that.

Before you know it, you'll be IDing winter visitors like purple finches, common redpolls, Lapland longspurs, snow buntings or evening grosbeaks that may visit your region.

Getting started: It's easy to get started. You can begin by getting to know your backyard birds. Scan your trees. Winter birding can be as simple as scanning the trees and bushes near your home. Take your child, spouse, parent or friend along with you. Birding can be solitary or shared with others. Your partner may spot a bird you missed. Make it an adventure, Lanham says.

You can also join a local, state or national birding group. Do some research on the groups in your area. Your parks may offer birding opportunities led by naturalists or other experts. Many of these opportunities are free. Winter birding hikes are a great way to learn and get active in the cold months.

All you must do is look, but if you have the right gear, you have a better shot of identifying what you've seen.

Binoculars: I got started in birding with a pair of 8x28 Vortex Diamondbacks, which run between $100 and $200. They work great and have a lifetime warranty. I lost the rubber eyecups, and Vortex replaced them for free.

Swarovski EL binoculars with Swarovision are much more expensive but highly rated and tend to retain their value if you want to go to the top tier. The Swarovski EL binoculars can run as much as several thousand dollars, but you are investing in high quality.

Nikon Monarchs are also highly rated and more affordable. 8x42 Nikon Monarch 5s are around $300 and have great reviews.

Ideally, try to sample binoculars before you purchase them. Like most outdoor gear, what you like best is highly subjective. Overall, look for clear, crisp images, good weight, waterproofing and grip. Magnification and field of view are also important considerations, Lanham says.

Apps and Technology: Birding apps abound. There are plenty of free and paid apps to choose from as well. Audubon, Merlin and eBird are good options. Some birders also like to carry print field guides, which are also abundant and varied. Local and regional field guides can be a good selection as well.

There are social media groups devoted to birding. These range from state birding groups to backyard birding groups. Such groups' intensity level varies, but most are welcoming to new and experienced birders alike.

Check out the groups your state and region have to offer. Ohio has Facebook groups devoted to birding like Birding Ohio, Ohio Backyard Birding and Ohio Chase Birds. Groups like these are a great way to see birds in your area. Each group typically has rules and etiquette for posting.

On an almost daily basis, someone is posting to a Facebook birding group about a rare bird sighting. This winter, snowy owls, evening grosbeaks, purple finches and common redpolls have been spotted all around Ohio. Often, rarities mingle in with the common birds. All you have to do is look.

Documenting/photographing species: Once you get started in birding, you will begin to understand the practice of listing birds you've seen.

Lanham recommends taking landscape and habitat photos with your phone, capturing the essence of where birds are at a given time. Start with a point-and-shoot camera, where the learning curve is relatively flat, and you can grow with the camera. Like binoculars, cameras range significantly in price and features.

Also, be respectful and follow the American Birding Association Code of Birding Ethics. This code includes respecting and promoting birds and their environment, respecting the birding community and its members and respecting the law and others' rights.

18

DOWNY WOODPECKER DOWN!

I was waiting out the first blizzard of 2014 in the warmth of my home when I heard a loud thump at my door. I wondered why anyone would be out in weather like this, but when I opened my front door, all I saw was an undisturbed blanket of snow. I surmised the noise must have come from the back instead. Olive, my ever-faithful corgi, was on high alert as we made our way to the back patio door. On my back steps, there was a male downy woodpecker, face-down and half-buried in the deep snow. Unfortunately, now I knew what made the thumping sound.

The woodpecker remained motionless for a moment or two, but then I saw it stir its wing a bit. I quickly threw on a heavy coat, boots and gloves and made my way to the backyard. I wasn't sure if it would survive or not, but I would do my best to help it.

The poor bird wasn't moving, so I gently picked it up, and it managed to compose itself a bit in my hand. I gently stroked its feathers as it blinked rapidly, trying to shake off the cobwebs. It was clearly dazed, but it sat gently in my hand and didn't seem at all concerned.

Cradling the little woodpecker in my gloves, I carefully made my way back around to the front door. Olive was surprisingly quiet as I made my way through the kitchen and toward the garage door. The bird seemed to perk up just a bit, but it still wasn't moving much.

I set up a little area for it in a big cardboard box in the garage, and it seemed content as I placed it down. As I paused to consider my next course of action, it shuffled its wings and flew directly to the garage door window. It landed softly and delicately on the curtain shading the window, undoubtedly having learned its lesson about impenetrable glass.

I carefully walked over and gently took the woodpecker in my hands again. I opened the garage door and trudged, a bird in the hand, to the wooden feeder that hangs from a maple tree in our front yard. I placed the bird on the feeder's perch; it sat still for a moment, seemingly gathering its thoughts before suddenly taking flight. As I lowered my hands, it flew quickly and gracefully out of sight.

Safe travels, little bird. I wish you well.

Part IV

CONNECTIONS
WITH THE EARTH

Andrew finding inner peace.

19

BLACK FRIDAY THE NATURAL WAY

While hordes of shoppers descended on the retail stores on Black Friday, I opted for the cold, quiet solitude of Punderson Lake in Newbury, Ohio. Standing in a long line of shoppers on a rare day off didn't sound very appealing; the only line I wanted to see was the one attached to my fishing rod.

I loaded up my gear and bundled up in some warm clothes and headed out just as the early morning light started to appear. With the heater blowing warmly, I made my way toward the lake to see if anything besides the wind was biting.

When I arrived at the lake, there wasn't a soul there except for me. The wind was whipping across the lake, and it was quite brisk, but the air had a nice, crisp feel that was not unpleasant.

I scouted out a few spots along the shore not yet covered with thin ice, and I casted a jig-minnow combo to see if any trout were lurking around the surface. Chickadees perched and chattered in the trees around me, probably wondering what the solitary figure on the half-frozen lake was trying to accomplish.

After thirty minutes or so, I realized I wasn't going to catch any fish, but I wasn't ready to head home, either. So, I stashed my fishing gear—although there was nobody there to hide it from—and found a trail that snaked along the shoreline. I uncapped my binoculars and began to hike.

The quiet solitude of the snowy woods seemed to relax my mind and revive my spirit. Then, a great blue heron, perched on a jagged, broken limb,

Winter view of Punderson Lake.

caught a glimpse of me and took flight—circling around the lake against the slate-gray sky.

I saw some interesting birds as I continued along the trail—a bright, red-bellied woodpecker, a tufted titmouse, a few juncos and a little nuthatch. They perched in trees or flitted about, blissfully unaware or unaffected by the cold and seemingly unconcerned about my presence.

Although I had no particular destination in sight when I began my hike, I found a tree stump after a few miles along the muddy trail and sat down to rest. I watched the quiet lake. I listened to the sound of the wind blowing through the trees. I saw the contrast of the bright white snow framed against the woods' dark trees and fallen leaves. I didn't have to stand in a long line or fight my way through an angry crowd to see these things—they were just there. They had always been there.

As I walked back to my car, I reflected on the many things for which I am thankful and grateful. I thought about my family, friends, job and the many blessings that I am fortunate enough to have.

I didn't spend a penny that Black Friday morning, yet I came home with peace, relaxation and rejuvenation. It was the best money I never spent.

20

On Silence, Peace
and Solitude

Throughout my life, I have experienced a few moments of perfect tranquility. Although difficult to describe, these quiet, peaceful moments are etched in my mind.

One such memory I have of peaceful silence was after a neighborhood snowball fight in the days of my youth. The battle had ended, and the kids were trotting off to their homes as the sky began to darken. I returned to my own house but passed the front door and kept trudging through the deep and heavy snow until I came to the backyard. I was sweaty and exhausted, so I found a spot to lie down in the crisp, white snow. While on my back, I simply stared upward into the vast expanse of sky above me. An incredible sense of peace and calm overcame me, a feeling of quiet comfort. It was as if time had stopped—just for a moment. It quickly restarted when I broke the spell by standing up and heading for the warmth of the house.

Another such experience of my youth occurred at my grandparents' house in rural Lexington, Ohio. I had spent the night, and I was up early and ready to fish. It was a bright morning, but there was a sense of rain in the air. My grandma gave me a hearty breakfast of thick, crispy bacon, heavily buttered wheat toast and eggs over easy. I bounded out the door with a full stomach and a smile on my face as I went out to try my luck at the neighbor's farm pond.

The pond was stocked with bass and bluegill, and over the years, I probably caught every fish in that pond dozens of times. This particular morning was exceptional; as soon as my bobber touched the calm surface of the water,

Top: The author with a Chagrin River steelhead trout he caught on a fly. *Gareth Thomas*.

Bottom: The Chagrin River on a bright, cold day.

Above: Great Blue Heron.

Left: Sunset on the Chagrin River.

Cooper's hawk in the snow.

Red-shouldered hawk.

Eastern bluebird during a soft snowfall.

Frog blending into its surroundings.

Prothonotary warbler.

Yellow-rumped warbler.

Above: Canada warbler.

Right: Black-throated green warbler.

Bay-breasted warbler.

American redstart.

Top: Chestnut-sided warbler.

Left: Toad on a wet day.

OBX sunrise.

Beartown Lakes reflections II.

Top: Ansel's Cave.

Bottom: Frog on the move.

Top: Winter hike.

Bottom: Reflective beauty.

Sign of spring.

Baby snapping turtle.

Left: Winter hike at Cuyahoga Valley National Park.

Below: Sunlight and water.

Above: Beach along the Atlantic Ocean.

Left: Andrew with a hefty largemouth bass.

Top: Spotted salamander.

Bottom: Swallowtail butterfly.

Above: Turtle posing on a log.

Left: Bird seed and sunlight.

Big tree.

it would dance and then disappear. I was having a fine time catching and releasing bluegill, pumpkinseed and the occasional largemouth bass. After an hour or so, a soft rain began to fall. I unpacked my grandpa's old raincoat that my grandma made me take, and I sat along the bank of the pond and watched the raindrops lightly touch the surface of the water. Again, a feeling of peace and serenity enveloped me, and I removed the raincoat and let the rain fall against my skin.

My most recent experience of silent tranquility occurred this very morning. I packed my fishing gear into my car, but on arriving at the river, I chose to forgo fishing and simply observe nature. (I also forgot to bring the bait, but that's another matter.) I walked along the shoreline of the Chagrin, and just as I arrived, two great blue herons flew overhead, casting prehistoric shadows over the river. Their massive wings made no sound as they rounded a bend and faded from my sight. I overturned a few stones where the bank met the water and found a salamander and a few crayfish, which scampered to find new cover. After fifteen minutes or so, I decided to leave the river and hike in the dense surrounding woods instead.

As I made my way through the woods, I began to feel a sense of peaceful solitude. It was not a lonely feeling, but it's a feeling I sometimes get when I'm alone. The woods were very quiet. The wind gently stirred the pine branches. A songbird's soft call floated down from some high perch. The river gurgled along in the distance. Perhaps the forest seems so quiet because life outside of it has become so loud.

I found a large pine tree with some sturdy, broken branches that I could reach. For some reason, I really wanted to climb this tree. I stood at the foot of the massive trunk, set my gear on the ground and began to work my way up the tree.

I stopped when I was about ten feet from the ground, as my desire to climb the tree did not outweigh my desire to survive if I should happen to fall out of it. I did manage to maneuver myself carefully, so I was lying on my back on a thick branch. From this spot, I could look upward into the seemingly endless tree above me. I was completely alone, and I had the opportunity to close my eyes and hear something very special. For just a moment, I heard nothing at all.

21

STARFISH IN MAINE

My wife, Amy, and I were married in September 2012. We had a beautiful ceremony and reception, and then we packed our things and made the long northeasterly drive up to Bar Harbor, Maine, for our honeymoon.

One of the main reasons we chose Maine was the idyllic natural beauty of the state, notably Acadia National Park. Neither of us had ever been to Maine, and we agreed it was the perfect place to spend our first week together as a married couple.

In the weeks preceding the honeymoon, we were dreaming about our trip when we were not planning the wedding. We received many brochures on things to see and do, but one image stood out to me in particular. On the cover of one of the brochures from Acadia National Park was a picture of a colorful starfish in a gleaming tide pool. When I saw that picture, it became very important to find a starfish on our trip. So, not being one to shy away from bold and outrageous declarations, I promised my bride-to-be that we would see a starfish by the end of our honeymoon.

We enjoyed a huge lobster dinner during our first night in Maine, and we made plans to explore Acadia National Park the next day. The national park was just about a mile or so away from our hotel, and early the next morning, after a delicious breakfast, we were off to explore the park.

Words do not adequately capture the beauty of Acadia. Worn and weathered wooden lobster traps lie broken and half-buried on the beach. Dense conifer forests intensify the majesty and mystery of Cadillac Mountain. Massive, solid blocks of pink granite stand unyielding against the bracing chop of the Atlantic Ocean. Exploring these monstrous granite slabs, which sometimes tower hundreds of feet above the rocky shore, is no trifling matter. One misstep by us, and death is a real possibility. We approached each hike with the reverence and care it deserved since neither of us cared to plummet to our doom.

We spent a portion of each day of our trip at Acadia, and each day brought new surprises. We spotted loons and seabirds bobbing in the ocean, hiked in woods so dense and soundless they would give Stephen King chills and felt the mist of the Atlantic against our skin as we carefully maneuvered along the granite walls.

The one thing that we did not find was a starfish.

I made it my duty to ensure we hiked at low tide, and I carefully examined each tide pool. We spotted some sea urchins, a few small crabs and some colorful sea plants, but there were no starfish to be seen. Given that it was so late in the year, I was resigned to the fact that finding one probably wasn't going to happen.

On the fourth day, I left Amy a few hundred feet above me and climbed down much farther than I had gone before. I had to stay low to the ground to keep my balance as I slowly made my way down the slick rocks. I saw a few tide pools along the way down but found them empty.

Just as I was turning around to come back, I noticed a crevice between two massive slabs of granite. As I looked down, I saw the bright sparkle of crystal-clear water. Something happened at that moment. It was simultaneous: a prayer and an answer. I already knew what I would see before I even saw it, and there it was.

It was a beautiful purple starfish, gliding slowly along the bottom of the shallow pool. I yelled for Amy, but she was already there behind me. I gently pulled the graceful creature out and placed it on a nearby rock so we could examine it more closely; it seemed to grip my hand lightly. I couldn't believe it; it was perfect. There was no soul around for as far as I could see, and I believe that moment was solely made for us.

I carefully returned the starfish to the pool, and as we made our return ascent, I noticed another tide pool. To our mutual disbelief, this one held a pink starfish. We watched it in silence as it slowly made its way toward the cover of the rocks. The next day we returned to the tide pools, but the starfish were gone. I was glad.

We made a simple wish, but it came true.

22

ON GARDENS
AND OTHER SIMPLE PLEASURES

Armed with tools and gloves,
I approach my winter-weary
flower beds on bended knees
hoping to get some new wine
from this old bottle, earth.
—*J.R. Whitehead, "The Seasons—Spring"*

Almost twenty years ago, my friend Ross Whitehead gave me a book of poems that he had written and collected in a short collection called *Eye of the Beholder: Poems about Gardens and Other Things.*

I always enjoyed Ross's poetry, though I appreciate it more today. On occasion, poetic images that appear in his book—the wind in a tree…a cultivating tool…an ancient oak—will pop into my mind for various reasons, particularly when I am outdoors. Today, for example, as Amy and I cleaned up the last of the weary, weather-beaten plants in our garden and harvested the final fruits of our labor, I heard Ross's words again: "Accept nature." We do.

Gardening is something that I have grown increasingly fond of over the years. To plant seeds, water them, watch them sprout into plants, watch the plants bear fruit and eat the fruit seems like a satisfying cycle to me. When the process has concluded, all that is left are the seeds. The seeds then return to the earth, and the cycle begins anew. At least that's the theory, although it rarely turns out to be quite that simple. However, I have seen it

Garden.

happen, perhaps even once or twice in my own garden. Nevertheless, I still find gardening to be a soothing and gratifying endeavor.

There is probably an inherently ancient satisfaction in the process of gardening, something as primal as the process of hunting or fishing. To me, the pleasure of gardening is similar to the pleasure of fishing. Perhaps it is the hope of a great yield. Or, perhaps, it is the satisfaction of connecting with nature. True, it is not necessary for many who pursue gardening as a hobby; however, it is as necessary as any other endeavor that brings people happiness. Then again, some of the simplest things in life bring me happiness.

For example, I like to burn wood that falls from the trees in my yard in the fireplace, I like to eat vegetables that have grown and ripened in my garden and I like to catch fish that swim wild in the rivers and streams near my home. These gifts from the earth I do not own or possess, but I am able to experience them while I am here.

I am grateful for them, and I am grateful for the freedom that allows me to enjoy them.

23

FROM LITTLE PLANTS, MIGHTY PUMPKINS GROW

As the first glimpse of early morning sunlight began to slip through the blinds, my wife, Amy, and I were already awake and preparing to plant our yearly garden. It was one of those rare Northeast Ohio spring mornings where the sky was light blue and endless, and the bright sun made the dew sparkle on the rich green grass.

We had the supplies—the plants, the tools, the soil and the fertilizer—now we had to do the work. I hauled the forty-pound bags of potting soil to the backyard so Amy could start potting the flowers. It was my job to till the land. When I was a kid, I remember seeing a handwritten ad thumbtacked to the barbershop wall where I used to get my hair cut that read: "Garden Services: You Chill. I'll Till." It had the little strips of phone numbers that people could tear off if they were interested, and the phone numbers were almost always gone. I suppose there are two kinds of people in the world: Those who till and those who chill. I till.

After the rich garden soil, fertilizer and native soil (mostly yellow clay with some assorted rocks thrown in for good measure) were properly tilled, we began to plan the garden's layout. We have three garden beds that feature various vegetables, herbs and other native species.

In one bed, we planted only tomatoes. What can I say? I love tomatoes. Near this bed is an herb garden that features English thyme, Greek oregano, mint, garlic and peppermint. The other bed is the experimental garden. We planted four pepper plants—two hot and two mild. We also planted peanuts, celery, leeks and a Dill's Atlantic Giant Pumpkin plant. The peanuts and

Garden II.

pumpkin plant were my idea, in case you were curious. The pumpkins are said to grow to be potentially hundreds of pounds. Nothing would make me happier than growing a hundred-pound pumpkin, and I told Amy that we would find a way to get it to a county fair even if it bankrupts us. We had to table that conversation, though, because we had more planting to do.

Amy planted three spinach plants and three arugula plants in two wooden container gardens, and we potted all the flowers we had until the forty-pound bags of potting soil were gone. It was a hard day of work, but it was one of the most fun and satisfying days I can recall. Now we get to watch our garden grow.

As we worked, I felt very thankful that we are able to kneel to move rocks, dig in the soil and have a modest little garden. To me, there is little more satisfying than eating vegetables grown in our garden.

Later in the summer, when we are resting atop our giant pumpkin eating peanuts that we have pulled from the fertile earth, we'll know that all of our hard work was worth it.

After all, from tiny plants, mighty pumpkins grow.

24

FISHING IN GREECE

M any summers ago, on one of the long and endless summer days of my youth, my cousin and I were in the mountains of Greece fishing a scenic little river that snaked along a small village named Nestorio. Against a backdrop of mountains, the river meandered along a gravelly shoreline, and like many of the rivers featured in my fishing excursions, it seemed like the perfect place to catch some fish.

We were guided by a thirteen-year-old native who continually bragged about the river's purity. He claimed that to drink from the river was to enjoy the finest and purest water imaginable. Naturally, we didn't believe him, but sure enough, he knelt and took a long, refreshing drink of the water. My cousin and I were both impressed and agreed it was indeed a pure river—despite its obvious lack of fish.

We continued around a bend to see if the river's depth at any point became greater than six inches when we noticed a shepherd (complete with staff) off in the distance with his grazing sheep. When I look back on it, the scene stands out to me as ancient and almost biblical. In any case, we took it as a good omen and continued our journey along the river.

My cousin and I were both outfitted with cane poles and worms that we had dug ourselves. (In case you are wondering, Greek worms are very similar to American worms.) We kept fishing without luck in the hot afternoon sun, and I decided to walk farther upstream to see if I could scout out a better spot.

As I walked along the rocky shoreline, I came to a point where I had to cross the shallow river. This crossing was of little concern given the shallow depth and hot weather, so I stepped right into the gentle rippling current. To my surprise, I looked into the water and saw a sleek, silver fish next to a submerged branch. It seemed to be already dead, but I thought it would be a great trick to put it on my hook and pretend that I had caught it.

I bent down and slowly extended my hand to grab the fish when I noticed it was slowly moving. I had to squint against the glare of the sun on the river, but when I did, I saw that the fish was grasped by the fangs of a huge snake. In a flash, I remembered my grandfather's advice, which was something along the lines of try not to get bitten by a snake because most of them are venomous and you'll probably die.

I believe I did a complete backflip and landed on my feet and then skimmed across the surface of the water and through weeds, thorns and anything else in my path like a fan boat across the Everglades. I am not even sure if my feet touched the water, but I would spend the rest of the excursion far from the fangs of that serpent.

The rest of the afternoon was pretty uneventful, except we did manage to catch about a dozen small fish. I brought these fish home to my elderly aunt, and shocked doesn't quite adequately capture her surprise that we had caught fish in the river. Apparently, she had not spent much time around outdoorspeople like me.

To my surprise, she tossed the little fish in a large cast-iron skillet, drizzled them with olive oil and fried them up. Finally, she offered one to me; graciously, I passed, and then she proceeded to eat the fish—heads and all. I was happy to provide.

I knew then that fishing in Greece is not for the faint of heart, and I keep that lesson with me.

THE TALE OF THE TOAD

I was taking our corgi pup, Olive, on a leisurely tour through our backyard late this afternoon when we came upon a toad. However, this was no ordinary toad. OK, it was an ordinary toad, but it was facing extraordinary circumstances—at least by toad standards.

As I walked our puppy through the backyard wonderland of sights, sounds and curious smells, Olive, of course, was in her glory. She was trotting along, sprinting this way and that, stopping occasionally to roll in the dirt or to gnaw on a tree root. Then, suddenly, she stopped short and came to a complete standstill. I almost tripped over her, as I was deep in thought and not paying much attention to the scene unfolding before me. Suddenly, she nearly jerked the leash out of my hand, but I snatched it from midair before she could escape. As soon as I did, I realized what had caused all the excitement. A plump little toad was sitting right in the middle of the backyard.

Although the toad was minding its own business, Olive was not. She was beside herself, trying to get a closer look at the toad. She desperately wanted to meet it—or, more likely, eat it. She strained, pulled, twisted and nearly corkscrewed herself into the ground, but I wasn't going to let her near it.

After a few minutes of struggling, Olive finally turned her attention elsewhere, and I decided to have a look at the little fella myself.

The toad appeared to be healthy, but it wasn't trying to hop away from me. I found that peculiar, but as long as it was willing to sit still and pose, I decided to take a few close-up photos of it. The toad didn't seem to mind a bit, although it's difficult to read a toad's expression.

Anyway, I knew I didn't have much time to take my candid photos because Olive wouldn't stay distracted for very long. She had busied herself by finding a patch of clover to roll around in, but that was only a momentary diversion once she noticed me leaning down to photograph the toad. As soon as Olive began her mad dash toward us, the toad finally started slowly hopping away.

I noticed that its leaps were rather shaky, and I suspected something was wrong. As I looked more closely, I saw that it had a Band-Aid stuck to its leg. I have seen quite a few toads in my day, but I've never seen one in such a peculiar predicament. I knew I had to help it.

It's not exactly a simple task trying to keep twenty pounds of unadulterated puppy mayhem under control with one hand while trying to catch a toad with the other, but I was giving it my best shot. I kept lumbering after the toad while simultaneously trying to keep Olive at bay. I knew I could free it from its impediment, and although I just wanted to help it, the toad was probably wondering why these two giants kept chasing it. Newly motivated by our presence, it picked up its pace considerably. Band-Aid or not, this little toad really started moving, and it finally hopped into some heavy ground cover.

After catching up to it, I firmly grasped Olive's collar with my left hand, and I reached into the leafy cover with my right. Success! I felt the toad. Then the toad did what toads do when someone picks them up. That was not so successful. But no matter, I had the toad in my hand. Gently, I removed the Band-Aid and set the toad back down on the soft grass.

Without so much as a glance back, the toad hopped away toward the woods without even pausing, free again to hop without restraint. We watched it hop away until it disappeared into the woods unencumbered.

Then we said goodbye to the little toad and headed back toward the house.

Part V

THE KAYAK FISHING STORIES

BLIND ANGLER GEORGE TICE CLEARS HURDLES AND GIVES BACK

N ever give up."
Words to live by for George Tice, an army reservist and Desert Storm veteran. In 1991, near Saudi Arabia, Tice witnessed a helicopter crash and pulled the only survivor from the wreckage.

The aftermath of the accident haunted Tice and left him struggling with anxiety, depression and posttraumatic stress disorder. After his service, Tice needed a positive outlet to relax and ease his mind. He met a group of veterans who fish together, but weather and the distance to the water often kept Tice on dry land.

In 2017, Tice moved to Florida, "mostly for the fishing," he said. Good times didn't last. The same year, Tice lost his vision after undergoing heart surgery and surviving a series of strokes.

When he recovered, Tice searched the internet for veterans who fish, eventually finding the Southwest Florida Chapter of Heroes on the Water (HOW). HOW is a veteran's organization with a mission to help warriors relax, rehabilitate and reintegrate through kayak fishing and the outdoors.

Tice contacted HOW. "I told them I'm blind and explained I needed help." He was determined to paddle his own kayak.

Tice was not an experienced kayaker when he began; nonetheless, he turned down an offer to fish with another veteran in a tandem. "The first time I went out I was scared, but I wanted to go in my own kayak," Tice said. "I was very nervous, but I told myself, 'You can do this.'"

Now, Tice fishes solo with another angler nearby. His wingman helps Tice navigate and calls out casting distance. "My partner tells me how far to cast and what structure I'm targeting," Tice explained. A special GPS sends audio signals letting Tice know when he is entering shallow water.

For Tice, kayak fishing is an unbeatable experience.

"I fish by feel. My sense of hearing and touch are amazing." He says fishing out of a kayak is better than a boat. "I am immersed in the action."

Tice feels even better with a fish on the end of the line. He's caught some beauties, including tarpon, snook, redfish and black drum. His most memorable catch was a sea trout.

"The sea trout was special because it was a day of firsts," Tice recalled. He caught the fish during his first HOW event, his first fish in the kayak and his first catch with an artificial lure.

It was also his first fish with teeth. He winced, then laughed, "Now I slide my hand down the leader and use a lip gripper to release the fish."

According to Tice, the best part of kayak fishing is accessibility: "Almost anyone can fish from a kayak."

Recently, Tice fished several tournaments, and he's picking up sponsors. His best finish is tenth out of seventy-six anglers. At HOW's Take a Soldier Fishing event in Naples, Florida, Tice talked to other anglers about how he fishes. He considers competition an important part of his message.

"Tournaments show people even though I have a disability, I can still compete," Tice said.

As a result of his kayak fishing success, Tice hopes to work with other veterans and people with disabilities. He is active in fishing and veteran's communities and delivers motivational speeches. "I'm trying to improve people's lives," Tice said.

Tice's most often repeated words of advice are, "Don't sit around and feel sorry for yourself. Get out and do something enjoyable." Tice has gone through difficult challenges and had to adjust to a new way of life, but he finds peace on the water.

He knows kayak angling is great therapy.

"It's empowering to have control of the kayak and the fishing rod." Tice would love to help more veterans and people with disabilities get on the water.

"Trying new things is a little scary, but never give up."

27

Ten Easy Steps to Properly Catch-Photo-Release a Fish

After years of research, conservationists have developed the best method to release a fish. Richard Abrams, a biological administrator in Florida, has been spreading the message through outreach and education. Follow these rules for a safe and effective release.

1. Work Fast

Returning the fish to the water as quickly as possible is key to increasing survival. The fish's slime coat protects it from parasites. If you have to handle a fish, wet your hands first. A rubber-coated landing net protects the fish's slime and prevents tangled lures and lines.

2. Wet Hands

Ideally, keep the fish in the water. If lifting the fish, do not hang it vertically by the jaw. Fish swim horizontally; hanging vertically strains the fish's organs.

3. Photos

Keep the camera within reach. Hold the fish horizontally and support the weight. Best to take a photo of the fish without removing from the water.

4. Hooks

Use circle hooks or barbless hooks. Abrams has been promoting them for twenty years. Circle hooks are designed to stick in the jaw greater than 90 percent of the time.

Not only does this reduce foul or deep hooking, but circle hooks are easier to remove. No need to rear back and set the hook. Simply apply drag pressure and the hook finds its place.

5. DEHOOKING TOOLS
Use the right tool. Most anglers use pliers to remove a hook, but a special tool, called a dehooker, removes the hook without touching the fish.

6. INJURED FISH
Return an injured fish to the water, even if it likely won't survive. A bleeding or deep-hooked fish still has a better chance of recovering in the water than on the frying pan. Even if it doesn't survive, the fish could benefit other wildlife.

7. REVIVING FISH
A common mistake is rocking the fish back and forth to force water over the gills. Fish don't swim backward. Instead, move the fish in a figure-eight pattern or walk it along the bank.

8. RETRIEVING GEAR
If the hook is too deep to retrieve, cut the line as short as possible. This is especially important for toothy fish. Yanking the hook or aggressively removing it can cause injury. Most hooks rust quickly. Barbless hooks can often be disgorged.

9. RULES AND REGULATIONS
Bag limits, size limits and seasonal regulations exist to protect the fishery and ensure sustainability. When a fish is out of season, take extra care with catch and release.

10. STAY ALERT
Be aware of your surroundings. Don't become so engaged with handling the fish you lose sight of impending dangers. Maintain stability and clear the deck. Finally, look out for nearby predators waiting for an easy meal.

28

How Kristine Fischer Became a Full-Time Tournament Pro

Kristine Fischer has been outdoors and on the water since her childhood in Weeping Water, Nebraska. Family fishing tournaments introduced her to competition, and now she is turning her talents into a life on the road. "I've been taking steps toward this my entire life," she told me over the phone from Lake Kabetogama in northern Minnesota.

After a promising start in 2018, placing in the money in a half-dozen events, Fischer decided to leave the rat race and hit the road. "I cashed nine or ten checks last year," she joked, then added that winning money gave her confidence to turn pro. With more big-money events on the schedule, a growing band of tournament pros are going full time.

So, Fischer left her Pilates practice, bought an RV and hit the road with her partner, A.J. McWhorter. To supplement her tournament winnings, she freelances as a writer and consultant and maintains investment properties. "I'm a jack of all trades," she laughed.

When I asked how many states she's fished, Fischer laughed again: "Holy cow, I can't even count." In the past eight months, they have crossed the continent, hit dozens of states and fished some of the biggest tournaments. "We've been from south Texas to Canada and everywhere in between."

So far, 2019 had been a successful year. Fischer won the Hobie Bass Open and registered another first-place finish in the KBF Trail. She knows something about being first. Fischer is the first woman to win a national tournament and qualify for the Hobie Worlds. She admitted being the only female in the pro series can feel intimidating. "I am a rarity in a largely male-dominated sport, but if you put in the work, you're an angler," Fischer acknowledged.

One thing she doesn't seem to worry about is winning. "I am confident in my abilities, and my mental game is right," she insisted. After almost a year on the trail, Fischer has developed these skills to stay ahead of the pack.

Life on the trail isn't easy. She spends up to six days a week fishing. A typical week starts Tuesday and Wednesday traveling to the next event, prefixing Thursday and Friday, fish the tournament on Saturday and Sunday, then back on the road to the next stop.

Fischer loves the spontaneous and unstructured lifestyle of life on the road. "This fills us up," she said. The biggest challenges are finding time to make healthy meals and exercise. She half complained, "It's tough to take a long, hot shower in an RV."

Perseverance is one of Fischer's strongest points: "I believe in my abilities, and I don't let it bother me when a couple things go wrong." She told me about a wrestling match with a four-foot muskie ending with treble hooks in both her hands. Without a knife to perform surgery, her fishing partner used another hook to dig out the huge trebles. With a thunderstorm approaching, Fischer didn't want to miss the action, so she went back to fishing.

Fischer also feels strongly about finding purpose in her work by sharing her knowledge and expertise. "In the fall, I am helping with Women on the Water, where I will be teaching classes to female anglers as part of a three-day event."

Fischer wants to use her success to inspire and empower other anglers who feel intimidated. She holds herself up as an example, "I got into the sport on my own with less than $1,000 investment in a used kayak and some gear."

Fischer's advice for hopefuls looking to follow her lead is this: "I have failed and drawn blanks in tournaments, but I never let the fear of failure stop me. Fear is a binding thing. Don't be afraid to fail."

29

How Fishing for Salmon Shark Started the Big Game Craze

In 2006, Allen Sansano, Chris Mautino, Howard McKim and Allen Bushnell were riding on the back deck of a large fishing boat heading to La Paz, Mexico. The friends were expert anglers with years of experience. On the long ride, the conversation worked its way to the ultimate kayak fishing trip. What started as four buddies shooting the bull ended with the first legitimate monster fish on a kayak.

Howard McKim, one of the first kayak fishing guides, proposed the ideal trip would be catching giant salmon sharks in Alaska. After some convincing, the friends were hooked. They started making plans to intercept the pink salmon run in Valdez, Alaska.

In a phone interview over a decade later, Allen "Bushy" Bushnell remembered the draw of catching the first giant fish in a kayak. "Every two years, salmon sharks show up for the pink salmon run in Alaska," he explained. He remembered McKim describing huge sharks, up to five hundred pounds, gorging on migrating salmon. The crew put their heads together to devise a plan to catch salmon shark from kayaks.

The Trip

In 2007, the conversation became a reality. The friends arrived in Valdez and then loaded their kayaks and crew on a large fishing vessel named *Bold Eagle*. "We were surrounded by black rock, gray seas and gray sky; the setting wasn't beautiful," Bushnell remembered.

As the anglers dropped their boats in cold, gray water, they were surrounded by huge sharks swirling on the surface; Bushnell felt the rush of adrenaline as his heart raced. "I'm glad the doctor gave me a stress test before I left," he laughed.

The anglers used heavy tackle, two-hundred-pound test, expensive reels and long wire leaders handmade by the skipper. For bait, they used twenty-four-inch frozen pink salmon. McKim hooked up first. Bushnell said the group looked at each other and acknowledged, "This was going to be epic."

Bushnell dropped his bait and hooked a shark right away. He remembered the huge fish taking line fast, towing him sideways. "We were doing battle," he said.

The shark pulled Bushnell far from his friends and the mothership. When he reached deeper water, the fish shot straight down. Bushnell would winch up a few turns, and the huge shark would take his progress back. "Then it turned on its afterburners."

After an hour, the huge fish came to the surface. Although the goal was catch and release, Bushnell's shark died during the fight.

"We ate it. I didn't find it all that tasty; it was edible, but not great," Bushnell admitted. He ended up donating most of the meat after keeping enough for his family.

In the end, everyone caught one shark. They kept two sharks. McKim managed to secure his fish and release it without assistance, proving a solo kayaker could best a fish three times his size.

The Aftermath

Ultimately, most people measure fishing success in the size of the fish. "Back then, the salty characters didn't have a lot of respect for kayak anglers," Bushnell laughed. He said people often look at his kayak and ask about his biggest fish. "I tell them 450 pounds, how about you?" he chuckled.

For Bushnell, catching the salmon shark was the trip of a lifetime. "It was so much better with friends," he added. When the story hit fishing message boards around the world, the team's achievement was celebrated and lauded. "My contribution was good looks and a sense of humor," he laughed.

30

NINE STEPS TO GET INTO ADVENTURE FISHING

H ost of the YouTube series *Field Trips*, Robert Field has taken adventure fishing beyond a hobby; he has made suffering for his catch a job. Six years ago, the young marketing executive watched an online video of Drew Gregory's multiday trip fishing the Devils River in Texas. Field was hooked. When the video ended, Field's dream of wilderness adventure and freedom was born.

Although Field has a master's degree in finance, he felt a pull to return to the outdoors. Today, he tours the country in an RV, filming his experiences fishing the hottest and coldest destinations on earth.

In his first year on the road, Field produced 79 videos, lived in 20 states, traveled 19,000 miles and spent 120 days fishing. "The show received 6 million views in 50 countries," he said. People tune in to see Field survive and thrive in any fishing environment.

How does Field define adventure fishing? "The key is fishing places that are hard to reach."

On the Pecos River, Field was caught in a thunderstorm when lightning struck a cliff above his head. "I was blinded for a few seconds and couldn't hear for half an hour," he remembered.

Then there was the time he encountered a mountain lion and her cub. "I think I slept thirty minutes that night," he laughed.

On another trip, fishing turned from fun to survival. "We had to get in the kayaks and catch bass for food," he said. For Field, adventure fishing is more about the journey than the destination.

Field Trips isn't just a YouTube show about how to catch fish; the host puts as much emphasis on exploring new areas and meeting the locals. "I enjoy catching new fish and visiting new places, but I love learning about different cultures," Field added.

In addition to sharing tips and tricks to target local trophies, Field shares regional history, culture and food. "I've met some incredible people who are into the outdoors."

So, how can you get into adventure fishing? Field provided nine points to get you started:

1. No experience is needed. Adventure fishing is a state of mind.
2. Bring friends, especially if you're new to adventure fishing. Safety is in numbers, and so is adventure. Sharing the adventure with a friend provides a witness to the experience.
3. Scout out a new location—it can be close to home. While many of Field's adventures are off the beaten track, he also finds new water to explore in urban areas.
4. Travel light—carry only the essential supplies. When dragging, lowering, lifting and carrying your way to the fish, every pound counts.
5. Plan to live in your kayak, to reach the most remote locations, set up camps along the way.
6. Practice self-sustainability. For real adventure, leave the mac-and-cheese at home and plan to survive on your catch.
7. Share the view by bringing a camera. What's the point of pushing the limits if no one knows the story? Capture trials and triumphs.
8. For multi-day trips, pack paper maps of the area. Technology can fail.
9. Focus on the process, not the destination. Sit around the fire and enjoy sunsets. Slow down. Relax. Enjoy the journey, whether it's one mile or one thousand.

So, what are the rewards of adventure fishing? For Field, it's about being healthy, working hard and gaining personal growth from challenges. "Nobody is growing from convenience," Field said.

He recalled an incredibly difficult trip through the Adirondack Mountains in New York, "Probably the eight hardest physical days of my life."

After emerging on the other side, Field could sense a change: "I felt different. I felt a connection to the past and how people used to live."

While adventure fishing may be about the action, Field reminds us to take it easy and enjoy the process. "Ultimately, it's about the need to connect with the wilderness."

31

The True Value
of Fishing Licenses

M any anglers complain about buying a fishing license. Filling out the form is a hassle, shelling out money is excessive and the consequences are too harsh. But a deeper look into the fishing tax reveals a value greater than a few bucks and a couple minutes.

For example, in Ohio around the mid-1930s, a fishing license was optional. When the state began a focused stocking program, it shifted from voluntary to mandatory licenses.

In that time, the number of licenses jumped from 100,000 to 600,000. License programs have become popular to pay for access and conservation programs that benefit anglers. Understanding how the money is used will make buying a fishing license less painful.

Fishing licenses and conservation are linked. Licenses fund conservation efforts, stocking programs and research on native species.

Fishing license money also helps pay for access, amenities and law enforcement. Anglers, scientists, nonprofits, citizens, localities and other interested parties can lobby the state's license fund committee for money to support angler-friendly programs.

For many years, the plan worked well. But recently, license sales across the country have dropped.

According to Curtis Wagner, a fisheries management supervisor for Ohio, there has been a significant downtrend since the late 1980s. "We were selling 1.1 million licenses per year. But we've had a drop of 600,000 residential fishing licenses."

There are various reasons for the drop. He considers one of the keys to be the general downtrend in the number of Ohioans who go fishing, hunting and trapping. However, Wagner and others are working on creative new ways to market licenses and hopefully draw in more support.

"Society is changing. In the past four decades, we've lost a lot of fishing licenses." However, he noted that many people are interested in funding conservation, land and water acquisitions, as well as water access. Maybe birdwatchers, paddlers and other users would be willing to buy a license. "Polls and data show many people care about these things even if they are not fishing and hunting," Wagner pointed out.

To increase sales, Ohio is trying new ideas such as offering multiyear licenses and cost increases.

If license sales fall, then funding for important programs will also fall. According to a recent bill in the Ohio legislature, "Licenses improve Ohio's state fisheries hatcheries and fishing access; protect and improve access to fishing, hunting and trapping land; improve shooting ranges; and ensure a state wildlife officer in each county and on Lake Erie." Many people, not just anglers and hunters, care about these resources.

Another important benefit of purchasing a fishing license is tracking the number of anglers and mapping trends in demographics and participation. Each person who purchases a license fills out a form that helps managers understand the resource's users.

Across the country, government officials are working to find new ways to do more with less. So why do you need a fishing license? Purchasing a fishing license plays an important role in conservation projects that many anglers, hunters and outdoor enthusiasts appreciate.

32

Kayak Fishing Revolution

Captain Ken Daubert didn't want to just write a book, he wanted to start a fishing revolution. The author of the 2001 book *Kayakfishing: The Revolution* was the first writer to introduce the world to paddle fishing.

Today, Daubert is an accomplished fishing guide, taxidermist and custom lure designer. Two decades after his groundbreaking book, he reflects on his early days, the inspiration for the book and where he sees the sport going.

How Did You Get Interested in Kayak Fishing?

"I was guiding out of a jonboat, poling through the weeds with two clients, and a guy came floating by in a kayak. Fishing the heavy vegetation looked a lot easier with a kayak.

I had a beauty of a kayak forgotten in the corner of my garage. I had almost given the boat to a friend to get it out of the way. After my first trip, I didn't enjoy fishing out of a motorboat anymore.

Fishing is based on stealth, and nothing beats the stealth factor in a kayak. The custom lures I create work best when I don't spook the fish. So, a kayak fits the type of fishing I do."

WHY DID YOU WRITE *KAYAKFISHING: THE REVOLUTION?*

"The book came as a result of people checking out my website, which was among the first websites focusing on kayak fishing. I received tons of emails and messages. The number of people trying to get info about kayak fishing was overwhelming. After a while, I decided to write a book. I wanted to compile all the answers to their questions."

WHY DID YOU CALL KAYAK FISHING A REVOLUTION?

"Because that's what it was, a kayak fishing revolution. A lot of people in the outdoors industry were talking about the sport being a fad, and they weren't doing much with kayaks.

In those days, we were rigging our kayaks and mostly improvising. I felt the sport was going to take over. Everyone who had a jonboat would replace it with a kayak."

WHERE DO YOU SEE KAYAK FISHING GOING IN THE NEXT TWENTY YEARS?

"Haha, I quit thinking about the future of kayak fishing. I like the simplicity. The sport is more complicated now. The simplicity is what lured me in. The kayak was a more accessible and more economical way to fish.

I still get out at least once a week. I am busy making lures, but if the fishing is good, I get out twice a week."

33

SUMMER KAYAK CATFISHING

All I could think about was dropping a line in the water, kicking back and soaking up the summer sun. It was the kind of hot and lazy summer morning that used to stretch out forever when I was a kid—a perfect day to fish.

I spent considerable time organizing my gear, ensuring that everything was neat and compartmentalized for the trip so I would have easy access to it. The body of water I was fishing, a small private lake near my home, is my sanctuary for kayak angling. I loaded my gear and hauled the kayak down to the bank.

There wasn't a clear place to launch, so I made my way over the rocks and through some fairly deep and pungent mud until I was able to get my kayak afloat. The journey is part of the charm, though. I placed my rod in the rod holder, and as I did, I slipped and grabbed the rod for support.

More accurately, I grabbed the lure at the end of my line for support. It drove itself deeply into my index finger, causing me to straighten up quickly and inhale deeply.

Whew! That opened my eyes more quickly than my morning coffee. I gingerly removed the hook and noted that the wound was relatively minor, so I climbed aboard. At least I knew the hooks were sharp.

I pushed off into the placid water, enjoying the pleasant scenery and hot August weather. Paddling was a breeze, and I quickly established a nice, smooth stroke as I headed off toward a submerged tree to try for largemouth lurking near the underwater structure. I sent my plug sailing forth and had a few vicious strikes but couldn't hook one. I decided to switch to live bait instead.

I put a crawler on the end of a hook beneath a red-and-white bobber and enjoyed a nostalgic moment after hooking a feisty bluegill. I cast again, and the bobber was dragged downward and across the water. I set the hook and knew I had something bigger than a sunfish at the of my line.

It was a nice bullhead catfish. It put up a good fight, but I wrestled it alongside the kayak. I was able to remove the hook easily from its lip and released the fish without removing it from the water, not always the easiest task with catfish.

The sunfish were stealing my worms as quickly as I could bait the hook. I was going for another catfish, but the bluegill wouldn't allow the worm to sink that low before stripping my hook clean. I put a nice gob of worms on the hook and cast again. The bobber immediately dropped like an anchor, and I set the hook. This fish was a good one.

It was a fat bullhead. It fought valiantly and broke the water several times. I was impressed and decided I needed a quick picture of this one for posterity's sake. Just as I got it up to the kayak, it shook the hook and dropped into the kayak, and more specifically, onto my lap. I don't know if you ever had a thrashing catfish fall into your lap in a fairly confined area, but it's a rather intense situation. When I was a kid, I remember hearing the urban legend that catfish sting. They don't sting per se, but they do have very sharp and spiny fins. So, while catfish don't sting, they do stab. In my experience, that is equally unpleasant.

I somehow maneuvered myself from beneath the wild cat without overturning the small vessel. It fell from my lap onto the floor, and with a mighty shake of its tail, it sent the container of worms careening across the bottom of the kayak. While I was scrambling to gather the fish and get it back into the water, I noticed that my phone, water, and a sandwich I had just opened were all completely covered in the dirt my nightcrawlers had recently called home. I finally wrangled the angry serpent, which somehow writhed itself into my fishing bag, back into the lake.

In a matter of moments, my pristine kayak and organized gear were covered in worm dirt and fish slime. And so was I.

As I grabbed a handful of worms and dirt from the bottom of my new kayak and tried to return them to their container, I couldn't help but reflect that this is the best kind of fishing. There is no better way to pass a summer day.

Part VI

PRO TIPS
ON OUTDOOR SKILLS

34

Catch a Steelhead on the Fly

W hen it comes to fly-fishing for steelhead trout, professional guide and instructor Jeff Liskay knows his way around the rivers and tributaries flowing through Northeast Ohio. In fact, he was born and raised on the west side of Cleveland and first got his feet wet fishing for trout and salmon in 1971.

On October 28, around twenty interested steelhead anglers gathered to learn the fundamentals of the sport at Liskay's presentation "Steelhead on the Fly" at the Rocky River Reservation of the Cleveland Metroparks.

Liskay started the presentation by commenting on the nationally recognized, high-quality steelhead fisheries that have been established in Northeast Ohio.

"We are fortunate to call these our home waters. We have the opportunity to catch a steelhead after work. Some anglers travel great distances to have a chance to catch fish like these. We live nearby elite waters that provide so many angling opportunities," Liskay said.

Liskay's comprehensive presentation began with tips on understanding the water and how fish move, likening a river to a conveyor belt.

He differentiated between lake fishing and river fishing, stating, "Rivers are confined and intimate spaces for fish. Steelhead are constantly moving as they work their way up and downstream. River conditions and water temperatures will often dictate the activity levels of the fish and where they can be found."

The next part of the presentation focused on the gear. 6, 7 or 8-weight fly rods are best for steelhead with a 10-foot, 7-weight rod being ideal. Reels should align to the weight of the fly rod and have a good drag system.

Liskay went on to discuss line, leaders, tippets, floats, knots, weights swivels and a wide variety of imitations for anglers to consider. He covered everything from fly-fishing beads to bits of yarn, all of which can produce a steelhead in the right conditions.

For Liskay, much of steelhead fishing comes down to what he terms the "Rule of Threes." The Rule of Threes applies to everything from water temperature (cold, medium, warm) to fly color (natural, dark, bright). The Rule of Threes covers just about every potential variable steelhead anglers may encounter on the water from the section of river they are fishing to the life stage of the fish.

The audience was engaged and interjected various questions about knots, fly selection and techniques. Liskay proved to have a wealth of information, which he shared freely and patiently with the group.

"There are no secrets in angling anymore," Liskay said. "We want people on the water, experiencing the beauty of this great fishery. That's the goal."

After the indoor presentation concluded, Liskay donned his waders and led the group down to the Rocky River for casting demonstrations and hands-on learning. The participants gathered around Liskay as he unpacked a wide variety of fly-fishing materials that he carries in his bag and shared tips on how to read and approach the water.

From the look of Liskay's effortless and accurate casts, it was clear that he had spent many years fly-fishing for steelhead. However, he also had some tips for novices.

1. Have patience and gain experience in the water. Success often takes time.
2. Consider hiring a guide to shorten the learning curve.
3. Learn to read the USGS river gauge and others (found online) to find the best river conditions for fishing.
4. Don't be afraid to move around in the water. Don't spend the entire trip casting in one spot—especially if it's not producing.
5. Think about fly color, size and presentation depending on water conditions and clarity. Black flies and imitations work well in most water conditions, but think outside of the box, too.

When the instruction ended, the fishing began. Undoubtedly, on the water is where much of the true education of an angler occurs.

35

How to Fly-Fish for Walleyes at Night

F ishing guide Jeff Liskay likes a challenge. Which is why, fifteen years ago, he started targeting walleyes at night—with fly-fishing tackle. "I like chasing a variety of fish with a fly rod that I would typically catch with conventional gear," Liskay said. "I learned through experience that the walleye bite is better at night than during the day."

And Liskay isn't the only angler who has caught on to this unique fishery. Bradley Dunkle, the guide and owner of Wildwood Anglers, fly-fishes for twilight walleyes, too. "It's niche and not for the faint of heart," Dunkle said. "You think you have it figured out, and they humble you. It's like a puzzle you're trying to crack. It captivates you and keeps you guessing. It will keep you on your toes."

But when you do figure out the bite, Dunkle added that it "makes you feel like a rock star."

Between the two of them, these two Ohio experts have dialed in the tactics and techniques on how to fly-fish for walleyes at night—and they've shared them with us.

When and Where to Fly-Fish for Nighttime Walleyes

According to Liskay and Dunkle, spring and fall are the best seasons to target Lake Erie walleyes on the fly. In the spring, you'll catch more fish, and fall is the time to hunt for trophies. During these seasons, walleyes move closer to shore—in other words, within fly-casting range—to gorge on baitfish, such as gizzard shad and emerald shiners. Dunkle prefers to wait until the fall to chase the larger walleyes, but Liskay will begin fly-fishing for walleyes as early as April.

Liskay and Dunkle both fish on Lake Erie, which offers plenty of public access to shore anglers. They recommend scouting long piers, breakwalls and jetties. More specifically, Liskay likes to zero in on submerged structure and riprap, such as chunks of rocks that have broken off the breakwall, which attracts shad and shiners. If he can find a flat, stable platform where he can cast to that submerged structure, he'll fish there come evening.

Both guides advise arriving an hour or so before sunset to set up and practice your casting—but don't be surprised if you hook up during one of these twilight practice casts. Liskay said the best fishing often happens right at dusk. "If the bite doesn't happen then, the second wave may hit around 10:00 p.m. I will fish until around 11:00. After that, I usually call it."

Fly-Fishing Tactics for Nighttime Walleyes

Liskay and Dunkle agree that the best way to get acclimated to fly-fishing for walleyes at night is to not fish with fly tackle. At least, not right away.

They suggest beginners start with conventional gear so they can get a feel for where the fish are and what they're striking—and then pattern their fly-fishing approach from there. "Everything that I use fly fishing, I have learned first as a conventional angler," Liskay said. "It's pretty crucial to find a comfort zone when fly-fishing at night for walleye. I stand there like a soldier until they come to me."

Liskay makes long casts—forty to sixty feet—and fan-casts to cover more water. "I will work my way parallel to the rocks, where the walleyes are cruising for baitfish," he said. "The fish has to be able to see and feel the fly. I start with two-foot strips with really long pauses. I'll count two seconds and then retrieve it. Then I count four seconds. Remember that the dingier the water, the slower the approach should be."

Dunkle likes to use the wind and waves to his advantage. "When the line is getting knocked around by the waves and current," he said, "use a slow retrieve and let the water do some of the work. The involuntary motion of the fly in the presentation is pivotal." He added that keeping the fly in the top four to five feet of water is key to staying in the strike zone. Don't fish them near the bottom.

Once you come tight to a fish, Liskay recommends keep the drag loose. The intensity of the fight can vary, but he said, "Don't expect them to rip the rod from your hand like a steelhead."

When you are ready to land the fish, flick on your headlamp and grab your long-handled net.

"Walleyes often strike closer to the shore, so the slack running line can be an issue," according to Liskay. "In those cases, I hand-play the fish. Keep the rod to the side during the fight and high-stick it at the end right into the net."

Essential Gear

Liskay brings an 8- and 10-weight fly rod when he goes walleye fishing. He'll use a floating line with a sinking fly or an intermediate or sinking line with a floating fly. "When the water is clearer, a weighted fly with a floating line works really well," Liskay said. He prefers a 9-foot, 12-pound leader with a floating line, but will shorten the leader to $7\frac{1}{2}$ feet on an intermediate line and $4\frac{1}{2}$ feet on a sinking line. He says tippet is optional.

Dunkle prefers a 10-foot, 7-weight rod and also uses both floating and sinking lines. He will also bring a conventional rod and reel and some buddies along to share intel on patterning. Dunkle said he is often the one catching the fish with his fly rod when other tactics fail, drawing plenty of attention from conventional shore anglers trying to get a look at his fly.

Both guides favor larger flies with profiles between 3 and $6\frac{1}{2}$ inches. When considering the best flies to get started, Liskay likes Clouser Minnows, Game Changers and Deceivers. The color variations are unlimited, but he will use chartreuse and white, white and blue and black and red depending on the conditions and water clarity. He tries to pattern the fly based on the conventional approach that is working best.

Dunkle will fish BULKhead Double Deceivers, Zonkers and articulated Rabbit Strip Divers. As for colors, he prefers black, white, gray and silver and redheads with white bodies. Dunkle stressed the important of belly color since the walleyes are looking up at the fly. Orange and pink bellies work well.

Finally, Liskay recommends buying or making a stripping basket to manage the line and avoid getting tangled on the rocks or pier. It will eliminate a lot of tangled frustrations.

36

Twelve Hot Patterns for Great Lakes Steelhead

The Great Lakes tributaries are a thriving fishery for a variety of different species—but no fish garners as much attention and obsession in the region as steelhead. Anglers travel from all over the country for a chance to hook up with these fish.

In terms of how to fish for steelhead, one of the most popular fishing tactics is on the fly. When you gear up for Great Lakes steelhead, a 6-, 7- or 8-weight fly rod works best. And make sure the reel has a reliable drag system. You're going to need it.

As for fly selection…

The go-to patterns that fishing guides throw often depends on variables, such as water conditions, time of year and angling pressure. We asked four experts to share their three essential steelhead flies that will catch fish in just about any conditions on tributaries of the Great Lakes.

Guide: Alberto Rey

Alberto Rey is professor, artist, author and professional guide in New York. He starts each Great Lakes steelhead season with a new crop of flies. "I think about it all year—what worked well, what did not," Rey said. "I go in with the approach that I'm going to make the perfect fly, the fly that catches the stubborn fish."

Fly No. 1—Cuban Flea

This pattern is visible below the water, which makes it easier to see when the fish decides to take the fly. "It's a little streamer that dances really well back and forth in the current," Rey said. "The fish don't have to make a snap decision on whether to strike or not right away. It doesn't slap the water. It stays and swims in a medium current."

How to Fish the Cuban Flea

"Drop the fly to simulate a bug falling off the bank or a tree," Ray said. "Once the fly drops into the current, do a mend. It's important to wait for the fly to drop into the current first—don't mend too quickly. Keep mending as needed to keep the fly in front of the fish."

Rey advises vibrating the rod so the fly seems to move in the current. The longer you keep it in the current, the better your odds. He prefers roll casting over back-casting because the line will often fall heavier with a back cast. Try to drop the fly gently and cause as little commotion as possible. An advantage to this fly is its visibility. "You can see it anywhere," he said. "When it disappears, set the hook."

Fly No. 2—Gray Zonker

For a more substantial, medium- to heavy-size fly, Rey likes to throw a Zonker. "I like gray," he said. "It's not super-light or too dark, and it has kind of a dirty body that doesn't spook the fish." This fly works well in a variety of water conditions. Rey also likes the action on the Zonker. "It pushes water and fills the space the way a baitfish would."

How to Fish the Zonker

Rod vibration is key here. "When the fly is moving through the current, I vibrate the rod," Rey said. "It makes the tail move likes it is swimming."

Fly No. 3—Red-Headed Blurple Leech

This leech is one of the darker flies in Rey's arsenal. It features a purple-and-black leech yarn body with a marabou tail to give it an enticing action in the water. Rey likes the thickness and chunky feel to the fly, particularly when coupled with a red conehead. The conehead really gets the attention of the fish.

How to Fish the Red-Headed Blurple Leech

"Cast it to the bank, wait a second for the fly to drop and make a quick mend," Rey said. "Because the fly gets so deep, it stays in the water on the mend. Keep the fly in front of the fish and control the speed of how it moves."

Rey likes to drop the fly just to the depth of being barely visible. "If the water is deep and the current is heavy, twitching the fly creates a sensitivity to strikes. If you feel a twitch in return, it's a good time to set the hook." He says to set the hook if you can't see the fly but feel even the slightest bite. Many times, the fish takes the fly and you will hardly feel it.

GUIDE: JULIE SZUR

Pennsylvania fishing guide Julie Szur loves sharing the wisdom and knowledge she's gained from a lifetime of fishing. For Szur, targeting Great Lakes steelhead is all about movement; the fish want to see the movement of the fly. Her advice is simple: Watch the water, watch the depth, don't get hung up on the bottom, make depth adjustments and don't fray the leader. Here are her go-to flies.

Fly No. 1—Brookie

Szur's signature fly has a special meaning for her. "I used to talk to Lefty Krey about designing something special," Szur said. "I wanted to create one that was meaningful to me. I always fish with my golden retriever, Brookie, so I designed a fly using her hair."

The Brookie looks and fishes like a minnow pattern. It has little eyes on the front, and when it's in the water, it vibrates and the tail flops around. In addition to the retriever hair, she will tie it using rainbow tinsel and Finn Raccoon in green or black on a size six hook.

How to Fish the Brookie

"Cast it out, count to five, and follow the fly using soft strips," she said. "Cast again and count down, sometimes using faster strips." Szur says dead-drifting a Brookie also works well.

Fly No. 2—Candy Egg

When a female steelhead is laying eggs, an egg pattern will almost always catch fish. And, according to Szur, she can't keep the fish off this particular egg pattern. This fly utilizes peachy yarn, and Szur likes to use a tangerine-and-peach mix of color, with a milky white vail over the edge and a blood dot in the middle. She ties this fly on a size 10 hook.

How to Fish the Candy Egg

"You have to have your split shot scattered if the fish are suspended or on the bottom," Szur said. "Most importantly, you want to make sure you keep the drift down, and you just have to mend and mend constantly." Szur will use a downstream cast. "I hold my arm straight and follow the fly straight downstream and bring it back upstream with a nice casting arc, moving my arm with the line."

Fly No. 3—Black or Golden Stone

Szur favors these stoneflies when the fish are first coming in and not yet ready for eggs. "The fly fluctuates in the water, and it twitches," Szur said. "Fish it when the water is gin clear for maximum effectiveness."

How to Fish the Black or Golden Stone

"Cast it upstream to the fish and keep a really tight line," she said. "It depends on how active they are. I may dead drift or give it a twitch to match the insects that are moving in the water." Adjust your approach based on the light conditions and movement of the water. These variables may dictate the activity of the fish and the approach. If the sun is high and bright and the water is clear, the fish will be easier to spook.

GUIDE: JEFF LISKAY

Jeff Liskay, a professional guide in Ohio, has been chasing Great Lakes steel for decades. He can talk to you about tactics that were used in the 1970s as well as what's hot today. Liskay will mix things up depending on where and when he's chasing chrome, but he has three standard flies that rarely miss.

Fly No. 1—Snelled Yarn

"I like the Snelled Yarn because it's so versatile, and it works," Liskay said. "I can change color and styles without cutting lines. I can make it small or big, within three hook sizes. I can do anything with it and switch things up on the water to adjust for water conditions and other variables." Snelled yarn is Liskay's go-to for egg patterns. "I've been snelling yarn since way back in the day," Liskay said. "Another great advantage is the yarn is on top of the hook, so I get a great hook-to-land ratio."

How to Fish Snelled Yarn

Liskay will begin with a box of precut yarn in a variety of colors cut ½- to ¾-inch long. Next, he runs his tippet from the swivel and ties his snell hook onto that. After he ties the snell on the hook, he leaves another 12 to 14 inches of tag end off the snell, and that's where he ties his dropper fly. "I'll fish it below an indicator with split shots on a dead drift," he said. "Smaller size hooks have shorter yarn in more subtle colors, while the larger hooks might have lengthier, brighter yarn. I always try to mix colors. Sometimes,

I'll run a nymph off the back. I rotate my approach. I'm always adjusting, always changing."

Fly No. 2—Fairyfly

"This fly catches them anywhere," he said. "It's an imitation of a caddis with a slight change of color we call a Fairyfly." Liskay likes chartreuse for stained or tannic water but will tone it down to lighter colors for clearer water. When the fishing pressure is high, he'll fish it blue and yellow. He ties a variety in advance to adjust to the water conditions.

How to Fish the Fairyfly

"Drop this fly in the buckets, and it will get down into the nooks and crannies," Liskay said. "It works particularly well fished underneath yarn as the point fly." It's a simple fly that he loves to use while guiding, mainly when fishing around structure. "I don't care if I lose 20 or 30 of these, so I fish them aggressively. By switching up the colors or going super small, scaling way down to 14 or 16, I'll get a fish on, and that will turn the key on a slow day." Casting closer to structure is key for these flies. "Six inches closer to the tree branches may be the difference between five fish and zero."

Fly No. 3—Synthetic Clouser

This fly is a minnow imitation with synthetic wings that will catch steelhead in any stretch of a Great Lakes trib. Liskay likes olives, blacks and tans upriver and minnow-white and copper down toward the lake.

How to Fish the Synthetic Clouser

"This pattern has more movement than a straight Clouser," he said. "I'll fish it under an indicator or fish it as the point fly on the very end of the dead drift and work it across the river on the swing. Look for the fish on the chase." Using this approach helps Liskay determine how aggressive the fish are that day. Warmer water temps typically mean more aggressive fish.

GUIDE: KARL WEIXLMANN

Karl Weixlmann is an author and professional guide in Pennsylvania. His fly selection approach is pragmatic, yet extremely effective. "I like to tie something consistent regardless of water conditions," Weixlmann said. "I love beautiful articulated streamers, but if a guy throws it up in a tree, I lose all those hours. As a guide, I want to tie something that won't take forever to make at the vice. Time is limited. Simplicity in fly tying is a savior."

Fly No. 1—Little Precious

According to Weixlmann, these streamer patterns are simple and easy to tie. They typically imitate an emerald shiner. "You can tie them big or small," he said. "It's my number-one streamer pattern. They work great on trout streams, too." Weixlmann likes to tie the pattern with olive on top and white underneath. "In dirtier water, I may throw some blue or flash in the middle," Weixlmann said.

How to Fish the Little Precious

"Steelhead are feeding heavily on schools of emerald shiners in Lake Erie," Weixlmann said. "You fish the conditions. Day in and day out, I think it's tough to beat the Little Precious. Just vary the colors." The Little Precious can be fished in a variety of techniques. Weixlmann will fish it under floats on a dead drift. "Just fling it and let it go. It's a phenomenal streamer off the beach."

Fly No. 2—Three Loop Pink Lady Egg

If you're fishing for Great Lakes steel, you'll want a few reliable egg patterns. Weixlmann's favorite is a Pink Lady, made from glo-bug skeins. He always ties it with chartreuse thread, which makes a big difference. "When it gets wet, and you hold it up to the light, it looks exactly like a spawn sack," Weixlmann said. "I pick out the one with the most tangerine-orange color that has a really light translucent, pink color. I like to fish opaque patterns."

How to Fish the Three Loop Pink Lady Egg

"I'll look to see where the fish are suspended," Weixlmann said. "Don't set up super deep. Start shallow and work your way into the deeper water. Fish will suspend in the long sloping pools. Drift with an indicator. Bottom-bounce it on a dead drift, and keep weight on the leader and stagger the shot. Pay attention to the end of the drift. Steelhead will often hit eggs on the swing."

Fly No. 3—Wiggle Stonefly Nymph

On Steelhead Alley, a good stonefly can out-fish an egg pattern in cold water, according to Weixlmann. "When water temps drop, if you're nymphing, you're going to catch more fish," he said. "For a general, all-purpose, nymph, I absolutely love a wiggle stonefly." What sets this fly apart from other nymph patterns is the articulated tail that wiggles in the slightest current. This fly requires a bit more time at the vice, but it's worth it. "It's not a quick, easy tie, but it's so effective."

How to Fish Wiggle Stonefly Nymph

"I use it in the winter in low clear water," Weixlmann said. "I'll fish that wiggle stonefly, really small, like 16s, underneath a dry fly. I'll drop it back to the deepest, slowest part of the pool in the darker water. Use it when they're hugging the bottom; it has a time and place. And it works."

37

HOW TO ICEFISH FOR GIANT WALLEYE, LAKE TROUT AND PERCH

As temperatures keep dropping, that means that the season's first layer of thick, fishable ice isn't far behind. For beginners, icefishing can be a daunting pursuit. Since you don't have the freedom and flexibility to motor from spot to spot, how do you know where to start on the ice?

No need to fret, because the three expert icefishing anglers in this chapter have you covered. Combined, they have decades of hard-water experience behind them, and they can help you figure out not only where to fish and what tactics to use—but also how to catch some of the biggest fish of your life.

ICEFISHING EXPERT: BRIAN BROSDAHL

Minnesota-based guide Brian Brosdahl—known simply as "Bro" in many fishing circles—is a multispecies expert. Here, he shares his best tips and techniques on how to fish for slab crappies, monster pike and beefy walleyes.

CRAPPIE | "For numbers, I really love to icefish shallow, healthy lakes on the weed edges and in the vegetation," Brosdahl said. "But the big slabs often lurk deep in the basins, wherever there is forage.

"For large crappies, I'll use a small spoon, like a Buck Shot Rattle Spoon in dark, stained water," he continued. "Remember that in some lakes, it's a finesse bite. I also like to fish jigs like the Mooska or a Mud Bug with a little tail or tipped with a minnow head or a wax worm." He likes to use a wiggle on the retrieve to mimic the motion of a baitfish. "Keep it above the fish. Don't set the hook in the middle of the school. Pluck the star off the Christmas tree. That way, their friends won't know."

Brosdahl uses 2- to 3-pound line for crappies. "In vegetation, you can go thicker, but open water will make heavier line stand out more. Don't use split shot or sinkers. These are big creatures, but their mouths are fragile. Just pluck them with a slight uptick when you set the hook. Be patient. You might just see a twitch. It's a very subtle bite."

Walleye | Brosdahl targets trophy walleyes in the late fall. Scout out areas of good walleye habitat like structure with weeds or rocks on top. Whitefish tend to spawn in these areas, and the walleye come in to chase the whitefish. "Chasing big ones is fun because they are as heavy as they're going to get," he said. "These early feeders are fat, and larger baits are the key." A big sucker minnow rigged on a 2.5-inch Buck Shot Rattle Spoon is a real walleye treat.

Brosdahl emphasized that you don't have to use a giant bait to catch walleye. You can also fish what he calls a Bloody Stump. Take a minnow and snip it just past the air sack so that it's still alive. Hook the minnow through the top of the nose and have it exit through the bottom of the jaw. "The carnage appeals to a walleye's predatory instincts," Brosdahl said. "When fish are aggressive, I'll use a whole lively minnow and jig the whole works."

"Another good technique is pounding the bottom of the basin and pulling up fast," he said. This strategy can get the big walleye cruising the bottom and trigger their instinct bite. "They have their instinctive lanes, but sometimes in deeper water, they'll suspend and feed up. Remember that walleyes can't always see it, but they can feel it. Start jigging at about six to eight feet deep for suspended walleyes and work it down. I like to drop it down and stir up the bottom because walleyes eat crayfish and frogs, too."

Northern Pike | "I like catching large pike—not the nuisance pike," Brosdahl said. "For big pike, I fish large lakes that have plenty of forage. Pike are fun because it's a different kind of fishing. I like to set lines because pike are usually not active. Try using sucker minnows or dead baits that are oily and stinky on a Northland Predator Rig. Big pike love oily, stinky baits."

Another technique Brosdahl uses is jigging a lively sucker minnow or jigging a big, fluttery spoon. He likes using colors like red and orange to imitate perch and bluegills. Something with a silvery or golden flash works, too.

Brosdahl says the pike bite is definitely a waiting game: "We've set up a portable couch and chairs and a fire pit. It's hard to be patient when you want them to bite now, but landing that trophy often requires patience."

ICEFISHING EXPERT: TIM MOORE

Tim Moore got hooked on icefishing by chasing smelt with his dad among the shanties dotting the Great Bay coves. For the past fourteen years, he's been guiding professionally on Lake Winnipesauke, in New Hampshire, and focusing on trophy white perch.

WHITE PERCH | Moore says that Lake Winnipesauke boasts some of the largest white perch in the country. "The average white perch in Winnipesauke is 12 to 14 inches, and many get up to two or three pounds," he said. "We call those jumbos."

Moore fishes with a 28-inch spinning rod and 4-pound line. He uses heavier test because he likes to get the fish up quickly. He says white clam-blade jigs work well in the clear water of Winnipesauke. "We use a single hook point tipped with a worm to get them going," he explained. "If they're finicky, we may tip with a maggot instead. After that, it's run and gun."

The strategy for jumbos is to hunt the basins. "White perch fishing translates well to striper fishing," Moore said. "They school up by size, they are nomadic, and they migrate to spawn. White perch work a school of bait, and some days you can go from nothing to 15 feet of fish below you in a matter of moments. The biggest fish tend to stay on the bottom or the outside of the school. Try to get on the bottom and retrieve with a slow, short cadence—use a tap, tap approach. Once one comes away, more will follow. Get that first one to bite, and it's game on."

ICEFISHING EXPERT: MIKE HOWE

Mike Howe is a Montana guide and outfitter who grew up loving anything that has to do with the outdoors. "Something about icefishing checks all the boxes for me," Howe said. "And if I had to choose one outdoor pursuit, my true passion is chasing monster lake trout."

Lake Trout | "Lake trout are large, aggressive predators," Howe said. "Number one, you have to have good electronics. I like to use a simple Vexilar flasher in really gnarly conditions." Howe fishes for big lake trout in sixty to two hundred feet of water. "A camera has limitations. It's important to understand maps and what the fish want. Look for major structure, cliffs, and drop-offs. We're fishing huge bodies of water."

"Lake trout spend time on the move looking for forage," he continued. "They're hunters. They'll camp on a school of fish, but they're constantly on the move." In terms of forage, lake trout eat cisco, whitefish and yellow perch. The essential baits Howe likes to have in his arsenal are heavy, flashy spoons like the Super Leech Spoon from Clam Outdoors. "I start with a heavy flutter spoon, with lots of weight, thump, vibration and flash. I don't tip it. I use it to gauge the movement and aggression of the trout."

Howe likes to hunt and catch the most aggressive fish in the pack first. "If I can take the biggest fish, the rest will fall in. If you're fishing as a team, while you're fighting the monster, start popping holes and drop down. Your buddy will get the second biggest."

If spoons aren't working, Howe likes tube jigs, particularly those with a few gashes and battle scars and scent in the body. "The more torn up the tube, the better it performs," he said. "Lakers tend to stun a baitfish. One or two lakers will shred through a school of baitfish. They will stun or injure them, and the biggest ones will pick off the injured."

Howe fishes with light tackle, even though 20-pound plus lakers are common. "You need something medium to medium-heavy—30- to 40-inch rods with some forgiveness," he said. "Braided line is a must with a fluorocarbon leader, especially while you're banging jigs."

Keep a tight line on lake trout because they can turn and move so fast. "That's the beauty of lake trout fishing," Howe says. "That fish is in control, and you're along for the ride."

38

SHOTGUN SAFETY

A Perfect Fall Day

I t's a crisp autumn morning, and it feels like it in Northeast Ohio. I'm on the road before first light with a steaming thermos of coffee by my side as I drive through the early-morning darkness.

I'm on my way to pick up my dad before we head out to New London for an Intro to Shotguns and Trap Shooting course presented by the Fitchville Conservation League (FCL) and Ohio Division of Wildlife.

My dad has a sparkle in his eyes as we load the old Ithaca and Winchester 12-gauge shotguns into the trunk of my SUV. It's been many years since we shot clays, and the refresher would do us both good.

Some of the nicest and most welcoming people I've met greet us at the door with hearty handshakes; those who love the outdoors are typically those kinds of people.

Men, women and children of all ages pack the long tables inside the club; in fact, there are quite a few children. Many are Girl Scouts—some are homeschooled, and all are eager to learn.

The course, while free to the public, was made possible by a grant. The FCL officers conducting the course were all volunteering their time and expertise to share their knowledge with the crowd.

The topics and course description, also available on the FCL website, included safe gun handling, home safety, range etiquette and tips on purchasing a shotgun. It also included live-fire training with an opportunity to shoot clay pigeons on the trap range, supervised by qualified instructors. All of the equipment was provided, including shells, with an option to bring your shotguns (which were inspected by an expert before use).

Tom Dunlap, president of FCL and retired from a long career in law enforcement, began the presentation with a specific focus on safety and proper firearm handling techniques. His pleasant and easygoing nature becomes serious when it comes to safety. It was the key takeaway of the morning.

Gary Bradt, vice president and former military, also did an expert job of walking the participants through the introductory elements of explaining and demonstrating parts and types of shotguns, among other topics, again with a strong emphasis on safety.

Regardless of one's experience or proficiency with firearms, it never hurts to review the foundational elements of safety and to respect the power of firearms. Gary and Tom have many years of combined military and law enforcement experience, and they have the stories to back up why a strong focus on the safe handling of firearms is critical.

Five key tips are as follows:

1. Muzzle safety is vitally important. Always ensure the gun is pointed in a safe direction. This is the responsibility of every person who ever picks up a firearm.
2. Treat every gun as if it were loaded, particularly when cleaning guns. Many accidents occur when a person assumes a gun is unloaded.
3. Be aware of the target and beyond. Ensure there is an appropriate backstop. Know that bullets are able to travel a long distance and through an animal—or the wall of a home.
4. Keep your finger off the trigger until you're ready to shoot. Some guns have safeties; some do not. Know your gun.
5. Wear your eye and ear protection. Hearing and vision loss can happen. Don't take your sight or hearing for granted.

A few other key tips involve reading and understanding owners' manuals, checking the barrel for obstructions, avoiding alcohol and drugs when shooting and keeping firearms locked up and safe.

After the good discussion and presentation, it was time to have some fun shooting clays on the trap range. The children had the first opportunity to yell, "Pull!" It was great to see an entire line of young women, all Girl Scouts, shooting clays with the help of trained experts. There were a lot of high fives and yells of encouragement that could still be heard through the ear protection.

After the kids had the opportunity to have several rounds of fun, my dad and I stepped up and took our turns. My dad busted the first three in a row against the bright blue sky, and it made me so happy to spend this time with him. It was a joy to shoot the old guns that had been locked away in the gun safe for too long. It was even more special to rekindle the memories of my youth and my dad's youth on a bright, sunny autumn day.

Check out the FCL and its comprehensive website for future courses. It offers a variety of classes for people of all ages and experience levels. Members are all too happy to share their knowledge and expertise with others.

We're all busy, but the seasons change quickly. Autumn days in Ohio are made for family and the outdoors. Get out there and have some fun before the snow flies.

39

TAKE SLAB CRAPPIES FOR A DIP

The definition of "slab" crappie differs by region. For some anglers, a 1½-pounder might qualify. For others, the title is reserved for crappies that bust the 3-pound mark. What doesn't differ by region is that spring is the peak time to get slabs on the line. Jack Canady and Brandon Fulgham have a combined fifty-plus years of guiding experience on two of the country's most well-known slab factories, and their tricks will help you weed out the little guys fast.

THE BIG DIPPER

Jack Canady, Woods and Water Guide Service
Home Waters: Kentucky and Barkley lakes, Kentucky

Canady has been fishing for crappies for more than forty years. Although he primarily leans on spider rigging from his boat, he knows that spring prespawn and spawning periods also offer shore-based anglers their best shot at slabs, and to catch them, being versed in long-pole dipping is a must. From March through early May, the fish will congregate in heavy cover, particularly brush piles, in relatively shallow water. Some may be reachable from the bank, but others will require wading, and a dipping approach allows you to get very close to the structure and lower a jig or live minnow straight down vertically into its heart. The trick to being effective is "going shopping," as Canady puts it.

"Dipping is an old-time technique that requires nothing more than a 10-foot pole, a spinning or a baitcasting reel, and a bobber," Canady said. "Dip the minnow or jig from one side of the structure to another. The key is dropping in tight cover without getting hung up. Move around the brush pile. If you keep hooking smaller fish, find another spot. Experiment with jig sizes and colors and suspend the bait at different depths to locate the big fish."

Landing a big slab with a long pole takes some finesse. Canady says if the bobber moves even slightly, assume the bait is in the crappie's mouth. When you set the hook, don't swing hard. In spring, runoff from feeder creeks and rivers often makes shallow shoreline areas of Kentucky and Barkley lakes muddy. If he's not using a minnow on a hook, Canady typically dips skirted tube-style jigs weighing 1/16 to 1/8 ounce. He says dark colors such as a black-and-chartreuse combo and olive are top producers in stained to dirty water.

THE SPIDER MAN

Brandon Fulgham, Grenada Lake Crappie Guides
Home Waters: Lake Grenada, Mississippi

Fulgham is a lifelong crappie angler who's been guiding professionally for more than a decade, and his home base of Lake Grenada is a particularly excellent destination for anglers with the singular goal of landing a true trophy slab.

"Sometimes I'll get clients who don't care about numbers. They just want the 3- to 4-pound fish," Fulgham said. "We might not catch as many on those trips, but it's very rewarding to help clients reach their trophy goals."

One reason why Grenada grows fish so big is that the winters aren't overly harsh in Mississippi. According to Fulgham, that equates to a longer growing season. Although he can find slabs year-round, spring is king, and spider rigging is Fulgham's technique of choice. This method of slow-trolling with up to twelve rods allows him to present minnows and jigs throughout the column while covering lots of water.

"We start in very shallow water—maybe 1 to 3 feet deep—and ease our way back to deeper water," Fulgham said. "If we're not finding the size we want, I might go as deep as 20 feet. Giant crappies are usually staged deeper and are more solitary than smaller fish."

Fulgham typically begins with just a minnow on a hook, though he might pin his minnows on 1/4-ounce skirted jigs to add color if he's not getting many bites. He keeps his boat speed around one-half a mile per hour; however, he's not afraid to give the throttle a nudge when the going's rough.

"When the bite is sluggish, a lot of people like to slow down," he said. "I do the opposite. I'll speed up a bit and try to trigger the fish's instinct to hit."

40

SMALLMOUTH ALLEY

The tributaries flowing into Lake Erie in Ohio, Pennsylvania and New York are known as Steelhead Alley. Each year, fly anglers from around the country flock to this region's rivers for the chance to hook up with a steelhead trout. From as early as September to as late as May, steelhead anglers can be found dotting the shorelines and wading the rivers. But when steelhead season dies down around mid-April, a different species is available in this fishery—smallmouth bass.

According to Dan Pribanic, owner of Chagrin River Outfitters in Chagrin Falls, Ohio, around this time of year, the region becomes Smallmouth Alley. Pribanic has been guiding excursions for smallmouth (and steelhead and other species) for years and has the expert take on this fishery.

The Grand River, Rocky River and Conneaut Creek in Ohio get a lot of ink for steelhead trout, and rightly so, but these rivers also produce good and trophy-sized smallmouth bass. In late April and May, the steelhead crowds clear out, and a fly angler has the opportunity to target smallmouth. During this time of year, it's not uncommon to catch a mixed bag of smallmouth and steelhead. Fish the top and middle of the runs for chrome, then head to the slow or still pools for the bronze beauties affectionately known as "footballs" to some anglers for their size and shape.

At the end of steelhead season, many anglers might be getting their boats ready for summer or heading out to the golf course, but this is the time to put on those waders, get in the water and chase the smallmouth bite. It's an excellent opportunity to pursue a native sportfish without having to deal with huge crowds. The anglers who have fished them for years know the smallmouth battle is the reward, not to mention the potential trophy-sized fish. But the best part of all is it's a whole lot of fun.

"Every spring, the first few smallmouth bass you hook, you forget how strong they are," Pribanic said. "Pound for pound, smallmouth put up a better battle than steelhead. Between the two species, I'd take a six-pound smallmouth over a six-pound steelhead in a bar fight."

There are some likely reasons why this region isn't as well known to anglers for smallmouth fishing. "For one, there is a shorter window—and the fishing can be hit or miss," Pribanic said. But putting in the extra effort and being patient is worth it. "Wade around the rivers and hook up with a six or seven-pound smallmouth, and you'll see what you've been missing. If you like smallmouth, it ain't a bad place to try."

Another great thing about this smallmouth fishery is the lack of angler traffic, which can be challenging during peak steelhead season. Fewer anglers mean more opportunities to test new waters and explore. However, Pribanic would like to see smallmouth fishing in this region get more exposure.

"I'd love to see more people get into it," Pribanic said. "Smallmouth are a sought-after gamefish all around the country. It's also a great opportunity for waders and shore anglers to chase a native sportfish."

Pribanic's favorite river to fish for smallies is the Grand River in Ohio; he describes it as "packed," but most if not all of the Steelhead Alley rivers produce smallmouth around this time of year. Start targeting them specifically from mid-May through mid-June. That's a good month of solid fishing, but it's not nearly as lengthy as steelhead season, so there are fewer chances. A guide or experienced smallmouth angler can shorten the learning curve and help get a rookie on the fish more quickly.

There are a variety of ways to catch them. Smallmouth are primarily warm-water fish, and they can be caught throughout the day in the late morning, midafternoon and evening. In fact, Pribanic notes that they are often more active later in the day as the water warms. It's a good opportunity sleep in and still hit the peak fishing times on the river—or hit the water after work. What could be better?

Smallmouth are found in slower water than steelhead. Look for them inside slower seams, around log jams and big boulders. They're not typically in the fast water—slow or still water is where you want to target them. Smallmouth will be waiting to attack their prey—in this case, your fly.

Pribanic favors a 7- or 8-weight fly rod. Flies and classic smallmouth patterns, such as minnow and crayfish patterns, Game Changers and Circus

Peanuts all work. Pribanic also recommends trying swinging streamers and moving them around when the water is up to entice the bite.

Another fun approach is chasing the topwater bite. "We use a lot of poppers and Gurglers. Poppers are more aggressive in terms of approach, while Gurglers are up there, and they can see and feel it. It's not as loud or in their face," Pribanic said. "Fish poppers and Gurglers on a dead drift. Mend the line and wait for the connection." It takes some practice, but the key is patience.

So, what does it look and feel like when a smallmouth smashes a topwater fly? Surprisingly, different than one might suspect. The bites can be fierce, but they are often more subtle.

"The takes are different," Pribanic said. "The fly may disappear, and the next thing you know you've got a three-four pound smallie on the line, and you're in for some fun. Fish topwater drifts on the surface commotion where the water is broken a bit."

Overall, consider hitting Smallmouth Alley when steelhead season dies down and you're still itching for a worthy battle before the summer fun begins. And hit up a local fly shop in the region, too, for advice on hot flies and locations or to enlist the services of a guide to get you started. Once you hook into a feisty bronzeback on the fly, you'll see why smallmouth have carved out their own place in this dynamic fishery.

—— *Part VII* ——

CONCLUSION

Train tracks at Cuyahoga Valley National Park.

41

WALKING THE LINE

Finding Summer during COVID-19

When it's January in Northeast Ohio, distant dreams of sunshine, blue skies and salt water begin to take hold. The holidays are over, and the weather is bleak. But there is a glimmer of hope—summer vacation.

Our annual vacation spot is in the Outer Banks of North Carolina. My wife, Amy, researched a variety of different beach houses until she found one that had a unique history to it—Johnny Cash and June Carter Cash spent a summer there in 1989.

Well, that was an easy decision. I disappeared downstairs and returned with my *Classic Cash '88* CD. I was already dreaming of fishing for sea trout in the surf with Cash tunes playing the soundtrack of summer.

We were so excited. We decided to pay for the whole trip upfront as we knew there was no way we'd change our minds. After all, it wasn't like there would be a global pandemic that would threaten to cancel the trip and change life as we know it, right?

In March 2020, when COVID-19 rattled across America like the train outside Folsom Prison, our trip was the furthest thing from our minds. And although we were disappointed, we just hoped we could get a refund.

Thoughts of seashells, sea glass, sea trout drifted out to sea; we put our best-laid plans aside with them. We masked up, laid low and adapted to our new way of life during the global pandemic.

Then suddenly, a few days before our trip was scheduled, something interesting happened: the islands reopened. After considerable debate, we decided to go. We would be staying in a private, sanitized beach house, we

Right: Trying unsuccessfully to fish the raging **OBX** surf.

Below: Stormy day on the Outer Banks.

could still wear masks and practice social distancing and a week away from our home where we had spent the last three months in isolation sounded pretty darn appealing.

We made it down safely that afternoon and caught a beautiful sunset. It was quiet; the beach was empty. It was magnificent.

I love to fish salt water. The massive expanse of the ocean, the majesty and mystery of the waves calmly lapping against the shore are entrancing. But there was one other minor issue ahead for us on this trip: the night we hit the beach, so did Tropical Storm Arthur. Talk about breaks.

We survived the storm and vacationed safely without illness or other incident. The weather was rough, but I did cast more than once into the white churn of raging surf, without much luck. But the sea trout will still be there next year, and hopefully, we will be, too.

In the bedroom where we slept were pictures of Johnny and June Carter Cash. I couldn't help but think about "Walk the Line." It's a fine line, indeed. But rather than lament lousy weather and worse viruses, we photographed each sunrise, breathed the salt air and were grateful for our health and each other. I think that's what Johnny would have done, too.

Beartown Lakes reflections III.

About the Author

The author with a fly rod.

Dr. Andrew J. Pegman is a professor of English at Cuyahoga Community College in Ohio. His teaching and contributions in the classroom earned him the Distinguished Faculty Award from the American Association of Community Colleges. He's published in *National Geographic, Field & Stream, Outdoor Life, TROUT, The Drake, American Angler, Kayak Angler, Paddling Magazine, The Plain Dealer, Ohio Outdoor News, SUN Newspapers, Cleveland.com, The Ohio Cardinal, The House Wren* (Cleveland Audubon) and others. A story he wrote for *American Angler* was recognized in *The Best American Sports Writing 2020* as a Notable Selection, and the Outdoor Writers of Ohio Awards awarded him First Place for Magazine Writing in 2020, among other awards for magazine, internet and newspaper writing.